WOMEN IN
SCIENCE

Barbara McClintock

*Cytogeneticist and
Discoverer of
Mobile Genetic Elements*

Cavendish
Square

New York

Cathleen Small

To my genetic marvels: Christian, Theodore, and Samuel. You are simply perfect.

Published in 2017 by Cavendish Square Publishing, LLC
243 5th Avenue, Suite 136, New York, NY 10016

CPSIA Compliance Information: Batch #CW17CSQ

All websites were available and accurate when this book was sent to press.

Library of Congress Cataloging-in-Publication Data

Names: Small, Cathleen.
Title: Barbara McClintock: cytogeneticist and discoverer of mobile genetic elements / Cathleen Small.
Description: New York : Cavendish Square, 2017. | Series: Women in science | Includes index.
Identifiers: ISBN 9781502623119 (library bound) | ISBN 9781502623126 (ebook)
Subjects: LCSH: McClintock, Barbara, 1902-1992--Juvenile literature. | Geneticists--United States--Biography--Juvenile literature. | Nobel Prize winners--Biography--Juvenile literature.
Classification: LCC QH429.2.M38 S63 2017 | DDC 576.5'092--dc23

Editorial Director: David McNamara
Editor: Leah Tallon/Kristen Susienka
Copy Editor: Rebecca Rohan
Associate Art Director: Amy Greenan
Designer: Alan Sliwinski
Production Coordinator: Karol Szymczuk
Photo Research: J8 Media

The photographs in this book are used by permission and through the courtesy of: Cover Everett Collection/AGE Fotostock; (inset) Tatiana Shepeleva/Shutterstock.com; p. 1 (and throughout the book) Bereziuk/Shutterstock.com; p, 4 Bettmann/Getty Images; p. 8 Universal History Archive/UIG via Getty Images; p. 10 File:McClintock family 1907.jpg/Wikimedia Commons; p. 12 File:McClintock family.jpg/Wikimedia Commons; p. 14 Cold Spring Harbor Laboratory Archives, Used with permission from Marjorie M. Bhavnani; p. 17 Pius Lee/Shutterstock.com; p. 20 Photo Researchers/Alamy Stock Photo; p. 22 Hulton Archive/Getty Images; p. 26 Dorothea Lange/Library of Congress; p. 30 Walter Bibikow/Getty Images; p. 35 Hulton Archive/Getty Images; p. 39 Wolfgang Flamisch/Getty Images; pp. 42, 69, 100 Bettmann/Getty Images; p. 44 Pbroks13/File:Punnett Square.svg/Wikimedia Commons; p. 47 Arina P Habich/Shutterstock. com; p.54 Biophoto Associates/Getty Images; p. 66 Tom Middlemiss/AP Images; p. 72 Courtesy of The Jepson Herbaria Archives, University of California, Berkeley; p. 74, 89 Courtesy Cold Spring Harbor Laboratory Archives; p. 77 Pictorial Parade/ Archive Photos/Getty Images; p. 86 AP Images; p.94 Robert Knauft/Biology Pics/Getty Images; p. 97 Courtesy Nigel Holmes; p. 105 Andrew Toth/Getty Images; p. 106 Olympia Valla/EyeEm/Getty Images; p. 109 Andrew Brookes/Getty Images.

Printed in the United States of America

CONTENTS

Barbara McClintock, famous for discoveries
she made while studying maize genetics

INTRODUCTION

A BRIEF HISTORY OF BARBARA MCCLINTOCK

Barbara McClintock, one of the most important figures in the history of **cytogenetics**, actually lived in relative anonymity until 1983, when she was awarded a Nobel Prize in Physiology or Medicine. At that time, she was only the third woman to win an unshared Nobel Prize in science, and she was the first woman to do so in that particular category. The sciences were—and to a large extent still are—a primarily male-dominated field, so having a female scientist who spent her career quietly studying **maize** plants take the premier prize in the sciences was quite amazing.

But it really shouldn't be. Barbara McClintock's contributions to her field were nothing short of extraordinary. She was born when the field of genetics was just emerging, and she was responsible for some of the most important advances in cytogenetics in the twentieth century, including the identification of **ring chromosomes** and the breakage-fusion-bridge cycle, as well as the discovery of mobile genetic elements, or "jumping genes," as they were called.

McClintock's work with mobile genetic elements is what ultimately won her the Nobel Prize, but the accolade came nearly forty years after her initial discovery. For decades, fellow scientists had discarded her theories of **transposition**, and some even thought she was crazy. But McClintock quietly and without fanfare continued her research, and in the late 1970s, the veracity and value of her discovery became apparent when molecular geneticists recognized the same process that McClintock had tried to describe nearly four decades before. Using electron microscopes and examining cells at the molecular level, molecular geneticists were able to clearly see the very results that McClintock had found decades earlier, using much more primitive technology.

McClintock was interested in plant cytogenetics rather than **molecular biology**, but her discoveries about the nature and behavior of **chromosomes** and **genes** were invaluable to the research later molecular biologists have done with regard to chromosomal conditions, disease, and bacteria.

The reasons why McClintock's early discoveries of mobile genetic elements were cast aside can't be pinpointed with absolute accuracy. Some may have doubted the ability of a woman in that era to produce such an extraordinary finding, but more likely is the fact that McClintock's work was so incredibly complex that even trained scientists couldn't fully understand it. McClintock knew that and tried to simplify her findings, but they were still highly theoretical and incredibly complicated, so many in the field chose to ignore the results she kept trying to present. Eventually, McClintock simply gave up trying to present her findings and went about her work quietly, secure in the knowledge that she was correct in her hypotheses. The results her maize plants showed her were enough to convince her that even if the majority of the scientific community didn't believe her, she had made a very important discovery.

A lack of belief from her community wasn't about to cause her to lose faith in her work, and she had a few supporters who never doubted her even when the rest of the community did.

Barbara McClintock never wanted to be considered a feminist icon—she felt she was too outside the box to ever be any sort of role model for women. Yet despite her personal feelings about being a feminist, she was just that: she refused to accept that a woman could not be successful in a male-dominated field, and she refused to accept less than what her male colleagues had—not in terms of pay, but in terms of respect for her work. Her gender was relatively a nonissue in McClintock's eyes; she was first and foremost a scientist—and a brilliant one.

Barbara at the age of forty-five

CHAPTER ONE

THE EARLY LIFE OF BARBARA MCCLINTOCK

Barbara McClintock is remembered as the Nobel Prize–winning geneticist who discovered mobile genetic elements—a bit of a maverick who succeeded as a woman in a strongly male-dominated field in a time when few women even worked outside the home. However, her somewhat unconventional upbringing perhaps provides clues about the pioneering female scientist who was to come.

AN UNCONVENTIONAL CHILDHOOD

McClintock was born on June 16, 1902, right around the time when Gregor Mendel's earlier work in **heredity** in pea plants was being rediscovered and the science of genetics was being established. But McClintock wasn't born into a particularly scientific family. Her father, Thomas Henry McClintock, was a doctor born to Celtic immigrant parents, and her mother, Sara Handy McClintock, was a descendant of colonists who came over on the *Mayflower*.

Barbara (third from left) *and her siblings, circa 1907*

Sara's father disapproved of the marriage between the two, preferring that his daughter marry a man with a similar pedigree to hers, but the two married anyway in 1898 and quickly built a family of four children: Marjorie (born 1898), Mignon (born 1900), Eleanor (born 1902), and Tom (born 1904). If you're wondering where Barbara is in that lineup, the answer is third: Barbara was born Eleanor McClintock, but her parents changed her name when she was four months old after it became apparent that she didn't exactly fit the feminine name they had originally chosen for her. Barbara was a solitary, stoic baby who didn't require much attention, and her parents felt a more masculine name like Barbara was more fitting to her.

The family wasn't well off. Although Sara had grown up privileged, her father did not support her financially after her marriage, and Thomas, as a young doctor, didn't make much money. Sara taught piano lessons to bring in money and the family got by, but they didn't have any extra money. That, combined with having four children in a very short timeframe, put a lot of strain on Sara. She was unprepared for the challenges of raising four young children on a tight budget, and so she sent the child with whom she had the tensest relationship—Barbara—to stay with an aunt and uncle on Thomas's side for extended periods until she was school age.

This might seem a difficult prospect for a young child, but McClintock recalled the period fondly, saying, "I enjoyed myself immensely." Her uncle was a fish dealer and owned his own truck (unusual for those days), and McClintock often accompanied him on his work and watched with great interest as he worked on his truck. She had an early interest in tools and machinery, which further confounded her mother, who expected more traditional feminine interests from her daughter. Still, she assumed Barbara would eventually grow into more typical pursuits for her gender.

Mother and daughter were never particularly close—Barbara was reportedly a solitary child who didn't seek out physical affection, but neither did she have a particularly contentious relationship with her mother. Sara was known to fully support Barbara, even if she didn't always understand what drove her independent, nonconformist daughter.

At one point, Sara began to teach her daughter piano. However, she soon stopped because Barbara developed such an all-encompassing obsession with playing that her mother felt it bordered on unhealthy. Indeed, Barbara was known to be an intense child who applied herself with fierce passion to everything that interested her. She recalled this intensity actually interfering with her education on some occasions, telling biographer Evelyn Fox Keller, "This intensity or this sense of feeling disturbed about situations, or taking them too difficultly, led me to be taken out of school on several occasions."

Barbara (center) *with her siblings as their mother, Sara, plays the piano*

Luckily, this wasn't particularly an issue for McClintock's parents. They had a rather relaxed view of formal schooling, allowing their children to attend school or not as they chose. If the children had something they wished to pursue instead of school, they were permitted to take time off. And Thomas McClintock refused to have his children do homework, feeling that six hours of school time a day was plenty.

McClintock's parents had a similarly relaxed attitude about things like clothing. Young Barbara didn't care for the dresses and skirts that

LASER-SHARP FOCUS

The same intensity that Barbara had as a child, which led her parents to stop her piano lessons because they feared she was taking them too seriously, followed her into adulthood. At times, she would become so focused on a topic that she would lose track of everything else. While at Cornell, she once prepared heavily for a geology exam and was excited to take it—she knew she would pass it with flying colors because she had studied the material so intently. And indeed, she finished the test quickly, confident that she had done very well. There was just one small problem: She hadn't written her name on her exam, and she couldn't for the life of her remember it. She reportedly sat for twenty minutes, trying to remember her name, before it finally came to her and she wrote it on the test and turned it in.

As silly as the incident was, that intense level of focus would serve Barbara well in the decades to come, as she honed her scientific research. When she was studying a cell for the answers to a question or problem, her laser-sharp focus was certainly an asset.

McClintock during her time at Cornell University

Barbara McClintock: Cytogeneticist and Discoverer of Mobile Genetic Elements

girls wore and requested that she be allowed to have bloomers made to wear under her dress so she could climb trees and play sports with the boys in the neighborhood. Her parents readily agreed; Barbara said, "They always did acquiesce to anything that I wanted that they thought was important to me."

Barbara's mother did have concerns as her daughter grew into adolescence and didn't develop the usual interests she expected from a young woman, but in general, she allowed her quirky daughter to be herself.

A LOVE FOR SCIENCE

Although McClintock's father was a doctor, the family didn't eat, sleep, and breathe science. It was actually a nonissue in their household. Barbara's love of science grew from the classes she took at Erasmus Hall High School in New York. She found she loved the problem-solving aspect of science and delighted in solving problems in ways the instructor hadn't expected.

Her love of science remained as she began to think about college, much to her mother's dismay. Sara McClintock hoped her daughter would pursue a path toward marriage, and in that era it was thought that if a woman was too educated, she was unmarriageable. Of her mother's worries, Barbara said Sara was afraid she would become "a strange person, a person that didn't belong to society … She was even afraid I might become a college professor." It might seem silly now, but in those days women who wanted to get married did *not* pursue careers in higher academia. In fact, when Barbara later taught at the University of Missouri, she was threatened with being fired when a member of the faculty read an engagement announcement for a woman with the same name and mistakenly assumed it was for Barbara!

McClintock wasn't worried, though. She didn't have any interest in marriage; she hungered for knowledge and education, not for a family life. She resolved to "take the consequences for the sake of an activity that [she] knew would give [her] great pleasure"—furthering her education. If that meant no family, so be it. Said McClintock, "Whatever the consequences, *I had to go in that direction.*"

COLLEGE DAYS

Barbara did have to put aside her dreams of higher education temporarily. Her father had gone overseas to offer his services during World War I, and her mother did not support her desire to attend college. But when Thomas returned from the war in 1919, he supported Barbara's desire to attend college, and Sara capitulated. Not only did she stop trying to dissuade Barbara from attending college, she actually went out of her way to help her daughter get in. Barbara's sister commented, "Mother was most resourceful, and would have done everything necessary to see that Barbara was admitted, once the decision was made." Once again, Sara might not have understood her third child, but she supported her.

Barbara went to Cornell University, which had an inclusive vision of providing education to *all* students. There were other colleges specifically for women, but at that time the options for coed colleges were relatively limited. Cornell was one of the more inclusive universities, particularly for women interested in the sciences, and indeed Barbara found many opportunities there.

Not that the field was wide open, by any means. There were areas where women still weren't entirely welcomed. For example, the plant-breeding department wasn't admitting women into their graduate program at the time McClintock was a student. Instead, she had to enroll in the botany department, which *did* accept women. However,

Cornell University was a formative institution in McClintock's life.

she certainly had more opportunities than she would have had at many other universities, and she found she loved the atmosphere at Cornell, saying, "There were many things that one learned in college that one could not ordinarily learn then outside … College was a dream."

Much to everyone's surprise, solitary Barbara blossomed socially in her first year at school. She dated, she made friends, and she was even invited to join a sorority. However, when she recognized that a lot of young women were excluded from the sorority on what she felt were discriminatory practices, she refused the invitation to join. McClintock later told biographer Evelyn Fox Keller:

> **❝** *I just couldn't stand that kind of discrimination. It was so shocking that I never really got over it; even now I feel very strongly against honor societies. I belong to a number, because I have to if I have a job … [But] I just don't go to meetings.* **❞**

A SOLITARY SORT

Although her first year at college was a time of social blossoming for Barbara, she later reverted back to her naturally solitary tendencies. She stopped accepting dates, knowing that she had no intention of pursing a long-term relationship or marrying. She dove with great enthusiasm into her studies. She had friends and was reportedly well liked, but her general nature remained rather solitary. It suited her well.

Many people who are highly successful in a particular field have mentors or inspirations that have helped guide them along the way. Such was not the case with Barbara McClintock. Certainly, she drew inspiration from the work her fellow scientists were doing and had done, but she didn't cite any particular person as having initially inspired her love of science. When asked about mentors or personal heroes, she simply recalled that when she was a junior at Cornell, a professor invited her to take a graduate course in genetics, which she greatly enjoyed. From that point on, genetics was her field. She formed close working relationships and friendships with several other scientists in the department, and she spent her time doing what she loved—studying chromosomes in cells.

McClintock in her later years

CHAPTER TWO

THE TIMES OF BARBARA MCCLINTOCK

Barbara McClintock's life spanned most of the twentieth century—she was born not long after the century opened, and she died less than a decade before it closed. But her life's work was primarily done between the 1920s and the 1970s. It was a time of great fluctuation in the century, from the highs of the Roaring Twenties to the lows of the **Great Depression** and World War II, and then back to the highs of the **American Dream** and the lows of the Vietnam War era. The role of women fluctuated greatly during these time periods as well.

THE ROARING TWENTIES

In general, the 1920s was a time of great prosperity. World War I ended in 1918, and the United States and many other parts of the world experienced an economic boom in the years that followed.

Part of that boom was attributable to an industrial revolution of sorts, with growth and development in the fields of automobiles, electricity, and telephones, and the movie industry. That sort of growth

The Roaring Twenties was the era of flappers, parties, and dancing.

Barbara McClintock: Cytogeneticist and Discoverer of Mobile Genetic Elements

and development meant that job opportunities were plentiful and national optimism was high.

Concurrently, some opportunities were opening for women. They still had far fewer opportunities in general than men did—for example, relatively few women went to college, and few had careers outside of the home. But the times were changing in ways that allowed women to gain some more equal footing. For example, in 1920, the suffragist movement finally earned women the national right to vote when the Nineteenth Amendment to the US Constitution was passed. That right was the result of a long, hard-fought battle by generations of women.

Interestingly, the percentage of female students in higher education actually dropped during the 1920s, from 47 percent to 44 percent, according to *120 Years of American Education: A Statistical Portrait*, a study done by the National Center for Education Statistics. Enrollment had steadily risen at institutes of higher education in the United States from 1899 to 1930, but the ratio of women to men dropped during the 1920s and continued to drop in the 1930s. However, the proportion of women earning degrees grew during that same period. So fewer women were enrolling in college, but of those who did, more were earning degrees. However, these degrees were generally bachelor's and master's degrees—the number of women who earned **doctoral** degrees in the 1920s was quite low. The number rose, but it rose at a slower rate than the number of women earning bachelor's and master's degrees, and it accounted for a very small number of doctoral degrees earned.

This made it all the more impressive that Barbara McClintock earned a doctoral degree from an American university in 1927. Yet her journey to her PhD wasn't without a few bumps in the road—the first of which was her own mother. Although McClintock's mother supported her children in their pursuits, she was *not* thrilled with McClintock's wish to attend college. She had hoped her daughters would pursue the more traditional path of marriage and motherhood, and indeed, her first two daughters ultimately did.

But Barbara never had much of an interest in marriage. In fact, she dated a bit and even formed some emotional attachments to men, but she never considered marrying them, saying instead, "These attachments wouldn't have lasted … I was just not adjusted, never had been, to being closely associated with anybody … And I could never understand marriage." What she *really* wanted to do was attend college, but her mother initially refused to allow it, and her father was away serving in World War I. So Barbara had to bide her time and wait. Once her father returned and talked her mother into allowing Barbara to go to college, she immediately registered and became a student at Cornell University.

At the time that she attended Cornell, women were not officially admitted to the plant-breeding department for doctoral degrees, so instead of graduating with a degree in genetics, McClintock graduated with a doctoral degree in botany. The reasons for this discrimination are unclear, with some sources saying it was simply an issue of sexism and other sources saying it was likely more a matter of Cornell's policy to place students in departments where they felt they would be able to successfully place graduates in the professional world after they completed the program. Regardless of the reason, though, Barbara McClintock did earn her PhD in botany from Cornell University in 1927—an admirable feat.

The 1920s are often known as the Jazz Age and the era of **flappers** at Gatsby-esque parties and wealth. Socialites in fringed, knee-length dresses with bobbed hair are a representation commonly associated with the decade, but Barbara McClintock wasn't a part of that side of the Roaring Twenties. Rather, she focused on her studies and research and spent the decade building the beginnings of her personal career. As a student, she did bob her hair in the style of the 1920s, but it was *before* the style became popular, and it was for a wholly different reason than style—McClintock didn't want to bother with the upkeep of long hair anymore, so she had the local barber cut it off, and the change caused quite a fuss on campus! Far from the flapper dresses of the 1920s, too, McClintock instead went to a local tailor and had him make her pants, because they were much easier to wear while working in the field than dresses or skirts were.

The 1920s ended on a rather devastating note that was in stark contrast to the overall prosperity of the decade. The Wall Street crash of October 29, 1929 kicked off the Great Depression.

THE GREAT DEPRESSION

Coming on the tail end of the folly and optimism of the 1920s, the Great Depression began when the stock market crashed on a day known as Black Tuesday in 1929. There were still gains and developments in technology, particularly in the aviation and media industries, but where people had been enjoying wealth and prosperity, unemployment and poverty became the norm for a huge segment of the American population.

President Franklin D. Roosevelt enacted the programs of his New Deal, which were designed to stimulate economic relief and recovery, but it was a long, slow climb back to economic stability for much of the American public. Just like every other industry and field, the research field suffered. McClintock was finishing up her time at Cornell in the 1930s, and jobs and research opportunities were few and far between, thanks to the depressed economy. This, in part, led McClintock to take a less-than-ideal position at the University of Missouri, which turned out to be a difficult fit for her professionally, in part because the

The Dust Bowl of the Great Depression sent many people to California, where they lived out of their cars while working on farms.

conservative university saw no place for a woman on their permanent faculty in McClintock's department. She was denied promotions and isolated from the rest of her department at nearly every turn, although she did make favorable progress in her research while in Missouri.

Meanwhile, the depressed economy overseas allowed Hitler to make progress in advancing the agenda of the Nazi Party, and before long he began to lead an attempted takeover of European nations. It was a tense decade of the United States watching the goings-on in Europe and eventually stepping in to lend assistance. During this time, McClintock actually received a Guggenheim fellowship to work in Germany with a prestigious geneticist, but she ended up leaving after just four months, unable to stand the tensions going on in the country at that time.

Back on the domestic front, a drought led to the **Dust Bowl** of the 1930s, which caused major damage to crops in the US prairie states. Oklahoma and Texas were hit particularly hard, and tens of thousands of farming families in the region abandoned their devastated farms and migrated west to California, seeking work. Unfortunately, California's agricultural economy wasn't in much better shape than the Dust Bowl's, and many of the migrant workers who moved to California in search of work found themselves no better off than they had been in Texas and Oklahoma.

During this troubled time in history, Barbara McClintock was studying the genetic makeup and chromosome structure of maize— one of the very crops grown in the central United States, where the Dust Bowl was hitting farmers hard. But despite the drought and Dust Bowl, McClintock's career was on a positive trajectory, which mirrored the growing success of women during the 1930s. Although the entire economy was in a depression and opportunities were few, women were making progress in gaining recognition for their achievements. For example, Amelia Earhart is one well-known woman from the era. Her successes as a female aviator were admired and unmatched, and she gained a great deal of respect in a usually male-dominated field.

Barbara McClintock wasn't the public face that Amelia Earhart was, though. Her accomplishments during this time, though no less important, were known in a far smaller circle than Earhart's. A woman flying planes for long distances was exciting and noteworthy; a woman working in a laboratory on plant genetics was a bit less glamorous!

THE WAR YEARS

The beginning of the 1940s were war years for the United States. The United States officially entered World War II on December 7, 1941, after the Japanese attacked Pearl Harbor. It would be nearly four years before the war ended, and in that time, many Americans participated in the war effort. Men went off to fight on the front lines, and women worked overseas as nurses, for organizations such as the American Red Cross or as part of the United States Armed Forces. On the domestic front, women entered the workforce en masse, working in jobs vacated by men who had gone off to war. So although the war years were a time of death and devastation, they were also a time of prosperity for women, who began to enjoy workforce opportunities that had previously been unavailable to them.

The decade of the 1940s was a time of great change in American culture. Because of the number of women entering the workforce, it became more acceptable for women to pursue careers. Certainly, many women still opted to be homemakers who stayed home and raised the children, but the number of women opting for other opportunities increased dramatically. In 1940, the percentage of women in the American workforce was 27 percent; by 1945, that percentage had jumped to almost 37 percent. The famous Rosie the Riveter campaign was designed to recruit women into the workforce, and it was quite successful, though it didn't impact the poor wages for women, which were generally less than 50 percent of what men earned for the same job.

While women were gaining some success in the working world, though, Barbara McClintock was still hitting a **glass ceiling** in her career at the University of Missouri. The rest of the country might have been advancing in its views on women in the workforce, but at the University of Missouri, McClintock was underpaid, excluded from faculty meetings, and unable to secure **tenure**. Perhaps the warming climate toward women in the workforce gave McClintock some confidence when she decided to take a leave of absence from the University of Missouri and pursue other potential opportunities.

On the eve of Pearl Harbor, McClintock took steps to secure a temporary assignment at Cold Spring Harbor Laboratory in New York—an assignment that ultimately became a permanent position and home for McClintock. It was a position she debated not accepting, unsure of whether she was ready to settle into permanency there, but ultimately she did, and she spent the rest of her life at Cold Spring Harbor.

While working at the laboratory, McClintock continued growing her contributions to the field of plant genetics, and in 1944, she achieved the distinguished honor of being only the third woman ever elected to the National Academy of Sciences—an election that led the dean at the University of Missouri to try to lure her back. McClintock refused, well aware that she had no real future at the university.

Success continued for McClintock. By the end of the decade, she had also become the first female president of the Genetics Society of America.

McClintock spent many years of her working life at Cold Spring Harbor, New York.

THE AMERICAN DREAM YEARS

The late 1940s, after World War II ended, moved into the 1950s as a time of prosperity and the American Dream. When American men returned home from the war, they generally took back the place of head of the household and primary breadwinner. Many women returned to being homemakers and raising the children, and families began to move out to the suburbs. It was an interesting shift over the course of a few decades—in the 1930s, many rural-dwelling Americans had moved from agricultural areas into the cities, but by the 1950s, the appeal of city living began to dwindle for families as people moved out to suburban areas in the hopes of finding the perfect place to raise their children. The suburbs were almost a hybrid of the rural communities and the cities. Where the rural communities boasted farms and lots of land, and the cities had jobs and quick access to everything, the suburbs was sort of the best of both worlds—a place where a family could buy a house on a small plot of land and live away from the hustle and bustle of the city, but without the responsibilities of rural living.

This American Dream lifestyle wasn't for everyone, though. Some women had enjoyed their time in the workforce and remained in it, despite possibly having the opportunity to be a homemaker after the war. Naturally, this led to some tensions. First, some women held jobs that might otherwise have gone to men, and second, some men weren't comfortable with the idea of their wives working outside the home. In some cases, there was a careful dance as the genders struggled to find a new normal way of life.

But this was all rather a moot point to Barbara McClintock, who never married or had children. She had no husband to potentially resent her work, and she was in a field where there wasn't a lot of post-war competition. Few people were qualified to do the type of research she was doing, so it wasn't particularly a matter of men coming home from war and wanting her job, as would have been the case in many other industries.

Interestingly, Barbara McClintock stopped publishing the results of her work during the 1950s. Her work during this time was incredibly complex and not easily understood, even by her contemporaries in the sciences. Because she felt hostility and resistance from the scientific community, she simply stopped sharing her work. However, it did not harm her career. Normally, in academia and research, publishing is a key component, but the Carnegie Institution, which employed McClintock at Cold Spring Harbor, didn't pressure her to publish and instead allowed her to continue her research.

The reason McClintock stopped publishing was essentially a stonewall from the scientific community, which staunchly rejected the findings she produced in the late 1940s and early 1950s. Although McClintock was used to isolation, the rejection was frustrating and isolating, so she began to look for a change. She found it late in the 1950s, when she temporarily left the United States to study maize in Central and South America, pulling her further away from the strains of the American Dream that were taking place in the United States.

Plant genetics wasn't exactly a hot topic during the 1950s. At that time, the Cold War was beginning, and nuclear weapons were a very real threat. So a lot of scientific research and development centered around nuclear weapons and the "**space race**." Basically, the United States and the Soviet Union were engaged in a race to see who could develop the most effective nuclear weapons and technological superiority, and that race manifested itself in a focus on the development of space technology. So while Barbara McClintock continued her research and work on cytogenetics and plants, it didn't gain nearly as much attention as it might have if nuclear weapons and space technology hadn't been in the picture.

Aside from nuclear and space technology, molecular biology had begun to fascinate the next generation of scientists. A major scientific development of the decade was Francis Crick and James Watson's discovery of the structure of deoxyribonucleic acid, or **DNA**. This advance in molecular biology actually tied nicely into McClintock's

HEADING SOUTH

While Barbara McClintock was experiencing the chill of a stonewall from her scientific community, a bit of a crisis was taking place south of the border. The National Academy of Sciences discovered that the **indigenous** maize in Central and South America was in danger due to the growth and production of agricultural corn. McClintock was invited to train a group of local cytologists in how to collect and preserve the indigenous strains of maize.

It was quite a diversion for McClintock, who had spent the vast majority of her career in the United States—primarily in New York, Missouri, and California. The timing was good, though—McClintock's professional development was a bit stalled when the community discarded her ideas of mobile genetic elements, and certainly she was eminently qualified to train local cytologists on maize collection and preservation.

McClintock did that and more. In the two winters she spent in Central and South America, she trained the local cytologists as planned, but she also discovered that by studying the geographical distribution of certain chromosomal types of the maize, anthropologists could trace the biological history of the region's maize. This in turn would allow them to trace the migratory patterns of humans in the region, because reproduction of maize requires human intervention—maize can only grow where humans live because humans must aid in its propagation.

work in plant genetics, as both relate to heredity and inherited traits. At the time of Watson and Crick's discovery, however, McClintock was somewhat on the outs with the scientific community, and thus was continuing her own work in **cytology** quietly and without fanfare.

THE SWINGING SIXTIES

Although Barbara McClintock officially retired in 1967, she continued to work with graduate students at Cold Spring Harbor Laboratory after that time. Indeed, the 1960s and 1970s were decades of extensive research for McClintock and her colleagues. McClintock continued to work on the very theory that had gotten her shunned in the scientific community: transposition. But she worked quietly and without much notice, since the scientific community had no interest in what she was working on.

By this point in American history, far more opportunities were opening up for women. The 1960s brought about a breakdown in racist and sexist norms that had existed. No change happened overnight, of course, but the 1960s were a catalyst for many changes that positively impacted the role of women in society.

The decade brought about what some call the second wave of feminism. The first wave occurred decades earlier, during the women's suffrage movement. The second wave centered on, among numerous other issues, workplace equality for women. Books such as Betty Friedan's *The Feminine Mystique* challenged the role of woman as housewife and the notion of the American Dream, arguing that depictions of the American Dream limited possibilities for women.

The Equal Pay Act of 1963 attempted to ensure wage equality for women, stating that employers could not discriminate against employees by paying them lower wages based on gender. Although this sounded like an excellent plan in theory, in practice it was merely the first step

In the 1960s, women were frustrated over inequalities such as unequal pay, and some expressed their frustration at demonstrations like this one in New York City.

in a long battle. Women's pay did improve after the Equal Pay Act of 1963 in some cases, but there were loopholes that allowed employers to continue paying employees different amounts for the same job.

It was a good first step, even if now, some fifty years later, women still aren't earning equal wages to men. At the end of World War II, women were earning less than 50 percent of what men earned; by 2015, the wage gap was 21 percent, with women earning 79 cents for every dollar earned by a man, according to the Institute for Women's Policy Research. (Also according to the Institute for Women's Policy Research, it will take until approximately the year 2059 for women to reach equal pay to men.) Still, without the passage of the Equal Pay Act of 1963, it's likely that women would be earning considerably less than they are today.

Affirmative action came into being in the 1960s as well. It sought to ensure that job applicants couldn't be discriminated against based on a number of factors, one of which was gender. Like the Equal Pay Act, this was excellent in theory but somewhat less successful in practice. There are always loopholes that employers can use to discriminate if they so desire—in an ideal world, that wouldn't happen, but in the real world, employers can often find a way to hire the candidate they want, even if it means playing a bit loose with federal laws and regulations. Still, the fact that a company could no longer outright deny a woman employment based solely on the fact that she was a woman was a step in the right direction.

All of these issues—women's rights, equal pay, and affirmative action—could certainly have helped McClintock two decades earlier, when she was facing gender discrimination at the University of Missouri, but by the time they came about, she was quietly working at Cold Spring

Harbor, where her gender wasn't an issue, and her esteem was based solely on her work.

One prominent voice in the women's movement was that of Gloria Steinem. She was one of many voices to unite in the women's liberation movement, informally known as "women's lib."

While the battle for women's rights was going on, a Cold War was simmering. It had started in the 1950s, but it was still very much an issue in the 1960s. There was still the threat of either side using nuclear weapons to advance their agenda, leading both sides to focus on developing technologies in the space race. Plant genetics wasn't exactly at the forefront, though Barbara McClintock's research was still going strong.

While plant genetics specifically may not have been a hot topic in scientific research during the decade, medical genetics was gaining research ground. Doctors and researchers were anxious for new insight into chromosomal issues such as **Down syndrome**, inherited disorders, and the genetic developments that might provide insight into cancer and other diseases. The University of California, San Francisco (UCSF), for example, established its Division of Medical Genetics in 1967 and quickly dove into the emerging field. Earlier in the decade, 1961 brought the first screen for a metabolic defect in a newborn infant, when a doctor at Children's Hospital in Buffalo, New York, developed a newborn screening for phenylketonuria (**PKU**). This marked the beginnings of genetic testing, which is now commonplace not only for newborns but also prenatally, for babies still in the womb.

The work that Barbara McClintock did in plant cytogenetics most certainly influenced the researchers in the medical genetics research field. She may have been working on maize, but she was studying chromosomal structure, just as scientists in medical genetics were doing—and she had been doing it for decades. It took a while for scientists to realize that, though. In the 1960s, they were still largely ignoring her work, even though McClintock insisted that the discoveries she had made in plant genetics were applicable to all organisms. It wasn't until the next decade that her contributions began to be taken more seriously.

THE TUMULTUOUS SEVENTIES

The women's liberation movement continued into the 1970s, with women stepping increasingly more often into roles of power. The decade actually ended with the election of the United Kingdom's first female prime minister, a groundbreaking event for women worldwide.

However, the US economy was in a downturn, partly as a result of an oil crisis and widespread gas rationing, and politically, the nation was in upheaval. As the 1970s began, the United States was firmly entrenched in the Vietnam War, which was wildly unpopular with the American public. The Vietnam War, also called the Living Room War because it was so heavily televised in American homes, was one many Americans opposed. Many felt it was a battle America had no place in and that American troops were being sent overseas to a potentially deadly situation for no good reason.

The Vietnam War also bred mistrust in the government. Earlier in the war, the United States government had made claims suggesting that Americans were achieving success in Vietnam, that they were winning battles and making progress. In reality, however, the opposite was true. The South Vietnamese troops were no match for the North Vietnamese troops and the Viet Cong guerrillas, and even with the

McClintock's early discoveries when working with maize were precursors to the modern science that brought us GMO products such as corn.

American troops' help, South Vietnam was getting soundly beat in the battlefield.

The misrepresentation of the situation cost the American government a lot in terms of losing Americans' faith. Many in the American public became suspicious of the government, and the counterculture in particular became quite vocal about their wishes to end the war and about the fact that they did not trust the government.

Politically, it was a troubled time in America, but in terms of science, it was a time of discovery. The space program was going strong, with NASA having put the first American man on the moon in 1969. Stephen Hawking drove forward scientific research in physics with theories about black holes and Hawking radiation.

In the biological sciences, knowledge of chromosomes and DNA were instrumental in the advances made in genetic engineering. In fact, 1973 brought the first genetically modified organism (**GMO**), when the first GMO bacteria was generated. That was followed a year later by the first genetically modified mice. None of this would have been possible without Barbara McClintock's research into chromosomal structures and plant genetics—a fact that finally did not escape scientists. In the late 1970s, McClintock's earlier shunned work on transposition was being reexamined, and scientists began to realize the value of the research they had spent almost four decades overlooking.

It's interesting to realize that McClintock's groundbreaking research was in maize and laid the way for future developments in GMOs—one of the most prominent and controversial of which is currently corn or, as it's also called, maize.

THE EIGHTIES AND BEYOND

Barbara McClintock won the Nobel Prize in 1983, and certainly her contributions to the field of genetics are no longer overlooked. In the decades since, the advances in genetics have been too many to enumerate. New advances and discoveries related to genetics and heredity are occurring daily. Medical professionals are now able to establish a baby's genetic profile before it's even born, and enormous strides have been made in **prophylactic** measures to treat certain inherited conditions, such as specific hereditary types of breast and colon cancer.

McClintock wasn't a molecular geneticist, and she did not focus on diseases and human conditions, but her work with plant genetics informed the work of scientists who came after her and established a strong body of research and development in these fields.

At the age of eighty-one, McClintock
learned that she had won the Nobel Prize.

BARBARA MCCLINTOCK AND CYTOGENETICS

B arbara McClintock's contributions to the field of cytogenetics span approximately six decades, so providing an overview of her field is a rather daunting task. Yet the fact that she focused solely on maize makes it a bit more manageable—her contributions were numerous and her discoveries many, but they all focused on the seemingly innocuous maize plant and later provided valuable information to the greater field of genetic research.

A LITTLE BACKSTORY

To understand what spurred McClintock's interest in maize cytogenetics, we must think about those whose discoveries laid the building blocks in genetic research: most notably, Gregor Mendel and Thomas Hunt Morgan.

Gregor Mendel and Peas

In the mid-1800s, Austrian-born Gregor Johann Mendel, the father of modern genetics, was a monk in what is now the Czech Republic.

While gardening at the abbey where he lived, he began to experiment with pea plants and **crossbreed** them to achieve certain characteristics: height, pod and seed shape and color, and flower position and color.

Based on his experiments and ratios he found in his results, he determined that pea plants carried what he called **dominant** and **recessive traits**. For example, peas could be green or yellow, and Mendel found that if he crossbred a green pea plant with a yellow pea plant (the parent plants), the resulting peas (in the children plants) were yellow. But if he then bred those offspring plants, the green peas sometimes reappeared in the resulting grandchildren plants.

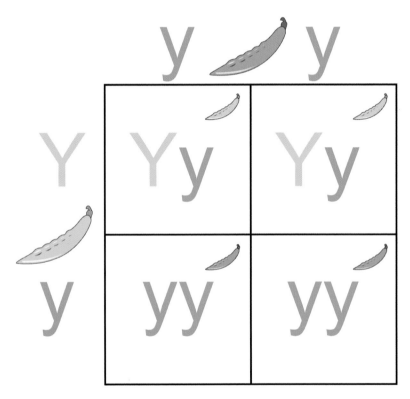

Dominant and recessive traits illustrated in a simple Punnett square. This shows that a yellow pea plant carrying a recessive green gene can, when bred with a green pea plant, result in either yellow (dominant) or green (recessive) child plants.

Mendel reasoned that the original yellow peas must be dominant, but their resulting yellow offspring (in the children plants) still carried a recessive gene for green peas, which could then reappear in the grandchildren plants if the crossbred plants each carried a recessive gene for green peas.

For a visual representation of dominant and recessive genes, it can be useful to create a **Punnett square**—a diagram designed by Reginald Punnett to provide a visual representation of **genotypes**.

In looking at the Punnett square, you can see that in reality, a green pea crossbred with a yellow pea *could* potentially produce a green pea, even in the child generation—it simply depends on whether the dominant yellow pea carries a recessive green gene in its genotype.

Much like Barbara McClintock's work, which often wasn't appreciated until years after her discoveries, not much attention was paid to Gregor Mendel's work at the time he did it. However, in later years the enormous significance of his discoveries became apparent, and he is now thought of as the father of modern genetics.

Thomas Hunt Morgan and Fruit Flies

One scientist who was influenced by Mendel's work was Thomas Hunt Morgan, who eventually won a Nobel Prize in Physiology or Medicine in 1933 and was an early supporter of Barbara McClintock's work.

Mendel's work began to be recognized for its importance in the early 1900s, and Morgan, a recent PhD graduate in zoology from Johns Hopkins University, began to study the principles of Mendelian genetics (not all of which he agreed with) with regard to the fruit fly, *Drosophila melanogaster*. The beauty of the fruit fly is its very short and prolific breeding cycle: a new generation matures from egg to adult roughly every ten days, and the female fruit fly lays about four hundred eggs over its roughly thirty-day lifespan. Scientists working with *Drosophila* can quickly see the results of their crossbreeding work and genetic study in each new generation born.

Morgan's life work in itself could fill a whole book, but suffice it to say that his experimentation and study led to the discovery that genes, which are carried on chromosomes, are the basis of heredity. This simple principle is the basis of genetics: living organisms have chromosomes, which carry genes, which determine hereditary traits.

One key difference in Morgan and McClintock, though, is that Morgan felt that genes were arranged in a linear fashion on chromosomes, whereas McClintock eventually came to embrace a theory of "jumping genes."

IDENTIFYING CHROMOSOMES IN MAIZE

When Barbara McClintock began her study of genetics at Cornell University, she quickly settled on maize as her area of interest. While Mendel had pea plants and Morgan had fruit flies, McClintock had maize. Why maize? Probably a number of reasons, not the least of which was that tuition to Cornell's College of Agriculture was free, and McClintock's family did not have an excess of money.

Also, while women were welcomed as students at Cornell, there were certain limitations in place. McClintock had taken a large number of courses in her first years at the university and had found herself drawn to science—in particular, to genetics, thanks to an exciting graduate-level genetics course that she had attended by special invitation from the professor. But genetics was offered as part of the plant-breeding department, which didn't accept women at the graduate level. So McClintock instead enrolled in graduate school in the botany department and specified a major in cytology to pursue her interest in

Early on, McClintock chose maize as the subject of her study.

chromosome work. She was also able to establish a minor in genetics and zoology. However, because her major course of study was technically in botany, it made more sense to focus on maize than on something like fruit flies.

Maize also intrigued McClintock because of its readily identifiable traits. The kernels of maize came in different colors and with different markings and different waxy surfaces. Maize's **phenotype** was distinctive and easily identifiable.

Further, in her first year of graduate school, McClintock had a paid position as an assistant to a cytologist in the department; under him, she had done work on maize chromosomes, which piqued her interest. In fact, this was where she made her first major discovery!

Scientists knew by then that maize, like fruit flies, had chromosomes, but they hadn't yet developed a good way to see the individual chromosomes in maize. Remember, this was before the days of electron microscopes, so it was up to the scientist to prepare, by hand, the clearest, cleanest slides possible.

The cytologist McClintock was working with had been working for quite a long time to try to isolate the individual chromosomes in maize on a slide, and McClintock found a way to do it in just a few days:

> **❝** *I had it done within two or three days—the whole thing done, clear, sharp, and nice. I never thought I was taking anything away from him; it didn't even occur to me. It was just exciting that here we could do it—we could tell one chromosome from another, and so easily!* **❞**

Perhaps not surprisingly, the cytologist's ego was a bit bruised at having been shown up by a young graduate student—and a woman, at that!—and the friendship between the two ended, but not before McClintock's discovery changed the future of microscopic examination of maize chromosomes.

The beauty of maize as opposed to fruit flies as an area of chromosomal study was that maize chromosomes were larger and thus, after McClintock's discovery, could be more easily examined. *Drosophila* chromosomes were so small that they really couldn't be seen well, even through a microscope. They could be seen, but not well enough to isolate specific structures on the individual chromosomes. Maize chromosomes, on the other hand, could be seen very well using McClintock's technique for slide preparation.

Scientists knew that maize carried ten chromosomes, but now they could isolate specific chromosomes by length, shape, and structure. They could even see specific, microscopic structures on the chromosomes, called **chromomeres**.

McClintock later used these structures and differences in chromosomes to help track genetic traits in crossbred maize, which she painstakingly controlled in the field to ensure purity of her samples.

According to Marcus Rhoades, a geneticist and close friend of McClintock's, this development meant that "[m]aize could now be used for detailed cytogenic analysis of a kind heretofore impossible with any organism." In other words, by simply altering slide preparation, McClintock had opened a major door in the world of genetics.

WORKING ON THE LINK BETWEEN CHROMOSOMES AND GENETICS

When McClintock finished her PhD at Cornell in 1927, she did not immediately move on. Rather, she stayed at Cornell to pursue a specific interest: She wanted to map linkage groups to particular chromosomes in maize. Linkage groups were sets of genes that appeared to be inherited together and were carried on specific chromosomes—scientists working on *Drosophila* had already established them in that species, but the study was difficult because, as mentioned, chromosomes from *Drosophila* were too small to study in great depth. McClintock wanted to do the same with maize, which provided chromosomes that were much easier to study in detail, so she stayed on at Cornell to work on that.

This is where McClintock met Marcus Rhoades, who would also devote his study to maize, as well as George Beadle, later a Nobel Prize–winning molecular geneticist. The three were sort of a "dream team" in research in maize genetics. Scientists in the field view this trio and their time at Cornell as the Golden Age of maize cytogenetics, and it lasted from 1928 to about 1935, during McClintock's and Rhoades's tenure at Cornell. McClintock said that it was "a piece of fine luck [that] a very fine group of graduate students came to Cornell at the same time."

Rhoades remembers of McClintock:

> **❝** *I recognized from the start that she was good, that she was much better than I was, and I didn't resent it at all ... It was so damn obvious: she was something special ... I've known a lot of famous scientists. But the only one I thought really was a genius was McClintock.* **❞**

During this Golden Age, McClintock's research work was growing by leaps. In a two-year span, she published nine papers on her research—quite prolific for a researcher! She had successfully mapped cytological markers on maize chromosomes to known genetic markers.

During this Golden Age, another notable female scientist joined McClintock's contemporaries in maize genetics at Cornell: Harriet

Creighton. Creighton was a young Wellesley graduate who arrived at Cornell for graduate study in 1929. McClintock took Creighton under her wing, and together the two worked on maize genetics. In particular, McClintock enlisted Creighton's help in proving the correlation between genetics and **chromosomal crossover.** Scientists had long assumed that child plants get their traits from combining traits from linked genes on the parent plants, but how this occurred hadn't yet been scientifically proven. By studying a particular knob on chromosome 9, which McClintock had isolated, through cycles of crossbreeding, Creighton and McClintock were able to prove their theory of how crossover occurs in a landmark paper published in 1931 in the *Proceedings of the National Academy of Sciences.*

Creighton and McClintock's paper was well received and gained the scientists positive attention in the field, but it would not have been so if Thomas Morgan hadn't stepped in. He was at Cornell to deliver a set of lectures when McClintock and Creighton shared their work with him. They had planned to confirm their results through another breeding cycle before publishing their findings, but Morgan intervened and insisted that they publish immediately. As it turned out, by publishing at Morgan's behest, the two female scientists essentially scooped scientist Curt Stern, who was about to publish his own very similar findings from his work with *Drosophila.* Creighton and McClintock were unaware of Stern's imminent presentation of his own findings, but Morgan wasn't— he knew about Stern's work when he urged Creighton and McClintock to publish theirs. Creighton said that when Morgan confessed to knowing about Stern's work, he said, "I thought it was about time that corn got a chance to beat *Drosophila!*" Because the breeding cycle of *Drosophila* was so short and maize's was comparatively long, it was a rare chance for maize genetics to shine.

RING CHROMOSOMES

Although the Golden Age of maize cytogenetics at Cornell lasted until around 1935, McClintock didn't stay for the entire time. She continued to do research there, but she also pursued other research avenues. In 1931, she began to desire a change. At that time, Cornell wasn't appointing women to full faculty positions, and McClintock wasn't willing to settle for less. She certainly could have taught for the university, but she wanted more—she wanted to be able to continue her research.

A two-year National Research Council fellowship gave her a needed change. McClintock still based her work at Cornell, but she also continued her research at the University of Missouri and at the California Institute of Technology. She crisscrossed the country in her Ford Model A, moving between the three locations.

The work at University of Missouri came about when McClintock's colleague and friend from her Cornell days, Lewis Stadler, extended her an invitation to do research at the university. Like McClintock, Stadler was interested in maize genetics—his focus was on mutations in maize genetics, particularly by X-rays. Mutations occur naturally when organisms reproduce, but exposing them to radiation through X-rays increased the number and type of mutations that occurred, providing an excellent basis for study.

McClintock was fascinated by Stadler's research and eager to work at the University of Missouri with him. Together, they irradiated the pollen of maize plants that carried certain dominant genes and then fertilized kernels from maize plants that carried recessive genes for the same traits. They found that the radiation introduced large-scale changes in the arrangement of chromosomes in the resulting plants. McClintock then worked to find the specific nature of the changes.

She ended up discovering **translocations**, inversions, and deletions in the chromosomes of the affected plants—all of which occurred when chromosomes exchanged genetic material during **meiosis**. Through her work during the summer of 1931, McClintock determined that when mutations occurred, sometimes certain genetic fragments would "get lost" and would cause a variation in the maize. She came up with the idea of a ring chromosome, which she felt was the opposite of a chromosomal deletion (where a fragment of a chromosome is missing):

❝ *If you had a chromosome that had two parts to it, you could invert [one] and get an inversion. Or you could get a deletion. At this point you say, well, the reverse of a deletion is a ring chromosome. Why weren't people reporting ring chromosomes? They weren't. Therefore, these ring chromosomes must have a mechanism of getting lost.* **❞**

In layman's terms, what McClintock believed was happening was that a piece of genetic material would break off a chromosome, and the ends of the broken piece would join together, forming a ring. Because of its unusual structure, that ring chromosome could no longer duplicate in the typical means, so it would get "lost" in the organism's genetic code—the deletion where the piece came from would be visible, of course, but the ring made from the broken piece would be virtually undetectable because it wouldn't reproduce.

The funny thing is, when McClintock came up with this idea of ring chromosomes, it was all in her head—she had never seen evidence of a ring chromosome in her slides. But in her excitement she talked to

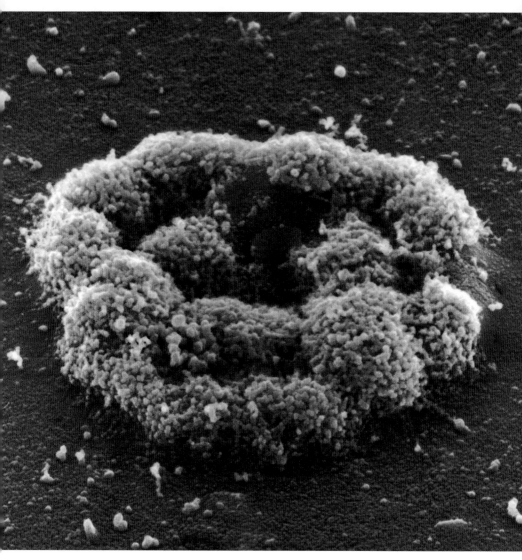

Electron microscopes can show proof that ring chromosomes exist, like this one from a Chinese hamster ovary cell.

her fellow researchers, who assumed she must be correct, because they didn't have any other rational explanation for what they were seeing—which was a set of variegated maize plants that seemed to stem from the plants bred during their experiments with X-ray and mutation.

McClintock panicked a bit when she realized her fellow researchers had adopted her theory without proof:

> ❝ *Then I got scared. I said, 'My goodness; they are now calling them ring chromosome plants when they have never seen a ring and don't know!' When the first plant was ready, my hand was actually shaking when I opened up the plant to get out the material to be examined.* ❞

Luckily for McClintock, her hypothesis was correct: Every plant she suspected to have a ring chromosome did indeed end up having one. It's a testament to McClintock's fellow scientists' belief in her that they took her assumption about ring chromosomes as truth. In recalling the situation, McClintock says she believed her theory and others did too because "the logic was compelling. The logic made itself, the logic was it." Indeed, logic informed all of McClintock's work over the years—the mark of a true scientist.

THE ORGANIZER

Not long after McClintock's discovery of ring chromosomes, she was working at the California Institute of Technology, still under her fellowship, when she became interested in a small piece of material at the end of chromosome 6. It was directly adjacent to the **nucleolus**, and McClintock had a hunch that the material had something to do with the nucleolus's development. "I found that this thing organized the materials that were already there to make the nucleolus. That's why I called it the nucleolar organizer," McClintock said.

McClintock studied the process of the formation of the nucleolus under her microscope and deduced that without that body of material on chromosome 6, the nucleolus would not be formed. It did, indeed, seem to be an organizer of sorts. Three decades later, scientists in molecular biology using electron microscopes would confirm her hypothesis, but the fact that McClintock saw through a simple microscope and accurately described the process was nothing short of amazing. In 1934, she published a paper of her findings entitled "The Relation of a Particular Chromosomal Element to the Development of the Nucleoli in *Zea mays*," and that paper is now considered a classic in the published history of cytogenetics. However, at the time the paper was not well received—McClintock claimed it was poorly written, and in any case the audience did not understand it. To be certain, it was a complicated subject that was difficult for scientists to grasp given that molecular biology had not yet become a field of study. (Molecular biology research would later reveal exactly what the organizer was doing to create the nucleolus, but at the time of McClintock's discovery, there was still much unknown. Scientists could tell *what* was happening, but not *why* or *how*.)

A BRIEF DIVERSION

When McClintock's fellowship ran out, she received a Guggenheim Fellowship to research in Germany. However, this was 1933, and Hitler was already in power—though not yet known for his atrocities. McClintock planned to work with Curt Stern in Germany, the very scientist whose work she had inadvertently "scooped" a few years prior. By this time, though, he had fled Germany, so McClintock planned to work with another well-known geneticist in the country, Richard B. Goldschmidt. His reputation in the genetics community was eventually quite colorful, thanks to his outspoken nature and his criticism of modern genetic theory, but at the time McClintock won her fellowship, he was held in high esteem.

However, their working relationship was not to last. McClintock left Germany after only four months, horrified at what she saw, particularly because she had many close friends who were Jewish. "It was a very, very traumatic experience," she said. "I was just unprepared for what I [found]."

THE MISSOURI YEARS

When McClintock's funding to do research at Cornell finally ran out in 1935, the country was in the grips of the Great Depression. Jobs were hard to come by, and jobs in research science were not immune. McClintock found herself adrift, wondering where to continue her research. Her best option seemed to be the University of Missouri, where her friend and colleague Lewis Stadler secured an assistant professor position for her. The position was technically below her, but McClintock took it anyway. Although she didn't particularly want to teach, the position allowed her to continue her research as well.

As it turned out, the University of Missouri wasn't a great fit for McClintock. Not only was she a female in a very much male-dominated field, but she was a maverick. Although McClintock didn't wish to be identified as a feminist role model, she very much wanted to be afforded the same opportunities as the men in her field—and she made that known. The University of Missouri was a quite conservative institution, and she wasn't exactly welcomed with open arms. Her department never informed McClintock of other institutions interested in hiring her, saying that she was due to be promoted at the University of Missouri, but she was never actually promoted. She was not invited to faculty meetings, and when she finally questioned the dean about her position, he informed her that if it weren't for Stadler's position at the university, she would be fired.

Despite the somewhat hostile environment at the university, McClintock made significant progress in her research. In particular, she furthered understanding of how broken chromosomes **reanneal**. Chromosomes have centromeres that are basically cell division poles. McClintock found that when broken chromosomes reanneal, they sometimes do so in an inverted fashion, which can lead to a chromosome with two centromeres instead of the usual one. This leads, during cell division, to a break in the **chromatin** "bridge" between the centromeres, and when the chromatin is broken, the broken ends then fuse with each other. McClintock called this cycle breakage-fusion-bridge, and when she published her findings about it in a series of papers, they were well received. McClintock's findings showed that this breakage-fusion-bridge cycle demonstrated where large-scale genetic mutations arose from, and scientists also felt that her work proved that the rejoining of chromosomes was not random but rather was determined by specific forces at work during cell division.

Although McClintock's work while at the university was promising and well received, she eventually was dismissed, in a roundabout way. The dean reportedly said that McClintock was a troublemaker, and that he hoped an offer would come up so she would leave. McClintock, knowing her presence at the university was not welcome, decided to take a leave of absence. She never returned.

Amusingly, though, she got the last word: After she left on her leave of absence, the dean found out that McClintock was being nominated for membership in the National Academy of Sciences—a very prestigious nomination, especially given that only two women had ever been elected. Suddenly, he became interested in retaining McClintock at the university. He even promised her a raise and promotion, which

McClintock refused. In her mind, "[T]here was no hope for a maverick like me to ever be at a university."

HOME AT LAST: THE COLD SPRING HARBOR YEARS

When McClintock left the University of Missouri, she was without a job, and the country was just entering World War II. Unsure of where to proceed, McClintock wrote to her friend and former colleague Marcus Rhoades. She knew he was newly installed at Columbia University, and she thought he might have some leads on where she could continue her maize research.

As it turned out, he did. He was going to continue his own research at Cold Spring Harbor on Long Island. McClintock decided to try to continue her research there as well, and she reached out to a fellow geneticist, Milislav Demerec, who had been at Cold Spring Harbor for two decades. He confirmed that she could come do her research there, and the rest is history—McClintock remained at Cold Spring Harbor until her death, continuing her research even long after her official retirement.

Although McClintock originally came to Cold Spring Harbor as a guest, rather than with an official job, it wasn't long before Demerec, who became the director of the Department of Genetics for the Carnegie Institution, offered McClintock a chance for a permanent position at Cold Spring Harbor. The offer included a home (small and lacking amenities, but McClintock spent most of her time in the lab anyway), a salary, space to grow corn, and a lab for research. It was a dream position, and McClintock didn't even have to take on any teaching duties!

She hesitated before accepting the position, not sure she was ready to be tied to it, but she ultimately took it, and Cold Spring Harbor became both work and home.

Around this time, molecular biology was taking off, and scientists were studying ever more minute, single-celled organisms, such as bacteria. Cytogenetics started to be pushed aside in favor of molecular research on subjects such as DNA, but McClintock stayed true to her passion and continued her research in maize genetics, even as she became more well known in the field. In addition to her election as a member of the National Academy of Sciences, in 1944 McClintock was elected the first female president of the Genetics Society of America, and she gained acclaim when she traveled to Stanford University to help her former colleague George Beadle unravel the genetic mystery of *Neurospora*, a type of mold.

While continuing her study of the breakage-fusion-bridge cycle at Cold Spring Harbor, McClintock made another startling discovery: transposition, or what many called "jumping genes."

McClintock was interested in the rate of mutation in maize, and she felt certain that something was controlling the rate, which was not always constant. It took a couple of years, but she patiently continued her research until she found what she had been missing: two components that she named the activator and the dissociator. She found that a certain component of a chromosome located adjacent to a gene would break, or dissociate, based on a signal sent out from another component that activated the break. Essentially, the dissociator took orders from the activator and dissociated accordingly.

That was the first piece of McClintock's discovery. Later, she found that this dissociation was merely part of a larger process, which came to be called transposition. In studying her maize crops, McClintock recognized a certain pattern of variegation that caused her to surmise that the dissociated genetic material was actually inserting itself in a new position on the chromosomes. What's more, she found that it was not only dissociators that could move around on chromosomes but also activators—the activator could tell itself to break and reattach! The dissociation and reattachment seemed to be controlled based on the "dose" of the activator present and varied based on the stage of cell development in which the dissociation occurred. What's more, McClintock felt that environmental factors could affect changes in the activator, which would then cause changes in the control of the dissociator and thus produce different mutations than expected.

By 1951, McClintock was ready to publicly present her findings about transposition. She had previously written reports for the Carnegie Institution, but they weren't widely read. She had shared her ideas with colleagues; several were supportive, but few truly understood her theory. To McClintock, the theory of transposition, activators, and dissociators made perfect sense. To other scientists, though, it was a completely foreign topic, and one they weren't eager to embrace.

In 1951, McClintock presented her findings at the Cold Spring Harbor Symposium. Her talk was a dismal failure. The scientists in attendance didn't understand her theory, and some even laughed, thinking she was a bit crazy in her ideas. One visiting geneticist at Cold Spring Harbor even told her, "I don't want to hear a thing about what you're doing. It may be interesting, but I understand it's kind of mad."

McClintock thought that perhaps she hadn't explained herself well enough, and she tried to present her findings in an article in the journal *Genetics*, entitled "Induction of Instability of Selected Loci in Maize," but the content was as inscrutable as the article title, and again she was met with confusion and disinterest. The same held true when she presented again at the 1956 Cold Spring Harbor Symposium; by then, her research had gotten even more complex, and her audience was even less inclined to buy into it. McClintock had a few supporters during this time, but not many.

At this point, McClintock stopped publishing her work. The Carnegie Institution didn't require her to publish, so she didn't. She grew to realize that she really didn't care either—she was happy just to do her work, regardless of whether the genetics community at large wanted to listen to her. She tried again to present her findings in 1960, after French biochemical geneticist Jacque Monod published with fellow French scientist François Jacob a paper on genetic regulatory mechanisms that mirrored McClintock's earlier theories on activators and dissociators. The molecular community, it seemed, was more open to accepting this theory than the genetic community had been. However, Monod and Jacob's success did nothing to bolster McClintock's theory, which was still shunned by her community. So, once again, she gave up on trying to convince her community of the validity of her theories.

The community's staunch refusal to consider McClintock's theory of transposition is most likely a result of two factors. First, the theories and research were so complex that many scientists couldn't truly understand them, no matter how skilled they were in their own field. Second, what McClintock was proposing with regard to transposition flew in the face of dominant genetic theory—that genes were fixed, unchanging units that determined heredity. The placement of genes on chromosomes had always been thought of as linear and fixed, but McClintock's work proved that wasn't always the case, that rearrangement was possible and, more importantly, not always the result of random mutation.

The scientific community's rejection of McClintock's theory was isolating for her. She had spent her whole life working in relative

THE NOBEL LECTURE

Winning the Nobel Prize is undoubtedly the greatest feather in any scientist's cap. It was especially momentous for Barbara McClintock because not only was she the first woman to win the prize alone in her category, but also some of her most important work had been ignored and even shunned for decades. With a characteristically positive outlook, McClintock had this to say during her Nobel Lecture, delivered in December 1983:

" *Because I became actively involved in the subject of genetics only twenty-one years after the rediscovery, in 1900, of Mendel's principles of heredity, and at a stage when acceptance of these principles was not general among biologists, I have had the pleasure of witnessing and experiencing the excitement created by revolutionary changes in genetic concepts that have occurred over the past sixty-odd years. I believe we are again experiencing such a revolution. It is altering our concepts of the genome: its component parts, their organizations, mobilities, and their modes of operation. Also, we are now better able to integrate activities of nuclear genomes with those of other components of a cell. Unquestionably, we will emerge from this revolutionary period with modified views of components of cells and how they operate, but only, however, to await the emergence of the next revolutionary phase that again will bring startling changes in concepts.* "

isolation—scientific research is naturally a rather isolated pursuit—but this shunning from her community was new to her. It did, however, prompt her to undertake a new venture, at least temporarily: She accepted an invitation from the National Academy of Sciences to go work in Central and South America training local cytologists to preserve the indigenous strains of maize, which were in danger of being lost due to agricultural corn spreading rapidly in the region.

While working there, McClintock realized that she could study the chromosomal types of the indigenous maize and, by doing so, trace the biological history of the native maize, which in turn would help anthropologists recreate human migratory history. Because maize only grows where humans live (due to how it fertilizes and reproduces), tracing the changes and patterns in chromosomes in the maize allowed McClintock to help trace a history of the corn, and thus the people of the region. Like her earlier work at Stanford with *Neurospora*, it was an interesting and useful diversion from her main body of research.

Ironically, while the interest in molecular biology may have been in part responsible for the lack of interest in McClintock's theory of transposition, it is also what ultimately drew people back to her theory in the 1970s. Advances in molecular biology began to show evidence of what McClintock had found in the late 1940s in her work on transposition. Small rumblings about McClintock's early work began to surface in the scientific community, but it wasn't until 1977 that McClintock's work really started to come back into focus, when Patricia Nevers and Heinz Saedler cited McClintock's work extensively in a paper they published comparing controlling elements in bacteria and in maize.

Better late than never. Once the importance of McClintock's work was realized, the accolades began to roll in, including the prestigious Nobel Prize in 1983.

HER ENTIRE BODY OF WORK

Barbara McClintock made countless contributions to the field of cytogenetics—far more than can be detailed in one chapter of a book. The major ones—ring chromosomes, the nucleolar organizer, and jumping genes—are probably what she'll be best remembered for, but certainly her entire field of research makes up a massive contribution to the overall study of cytogenetics and genetics in general.

McClintock was not overly comfortable with the press attention that arrived when she won the Nobel Prize.

CHAPTER FOUR

CONTEMPORARIES, CRITICISMS, AND CONTROVERSIES

Barbara McClintock was, by all accounts, both a nice person and occasionally a difficult one. She was a good listener who loved to talk about new ideas and concepts with her colleagues and students, but she was also an introvert who didn't suffer fools and who, on at least one occasion, threw visiting scientists out of her office because she couldn't stand their arrogance.

Although McClintock did not consider herself a feminist—in fact, she explicitly said she was *not* a feminist—she also did not take kindly to not being offered the same rights and opportunities as the men in her field, and she didn't hesitate to show her frustration when that occurred.

McClintock had no patience for discrimination. In college, she was invited to join a sorority, but she refused the offer when she learned that many of her classmates had been excluded.

When McClintock was strongly opposed to something, she let people know it—but then she went back to quietly doing her research. And so, she made waves, but in a way that didn't offend too many people. She was a pleasant person in general and reportedly got along well with the majority of her contemporaries. Like anyone, she had her detractors, but even more so she had supporters and colleagues who became lifelong friends.

INSPIRATIONS AND COLLEAGUES

Naturally, any geneticist is inspired by the work of Gregor Mendel, which started it all. But McClintock was more closely inspired by people who were working in the field at the same time she was, such as Thomas Hunt Morgan, Marcus Rhoades, George Beadle, and others.

Lester Sharp

Doubtless, one of McClintock's earliest influences in her study and research was Lester Sharp, a cytology professor at Cornell in the botany department. He was a mentor of sorts to McClintock, giving her private lessons in cytological techniques on Saturday mornings. She worked as his assistant, and he eventually became her thesis advisor at Cornell.

Their relationship was mutually beneficial. McClintock was a strong researcher, where Sharp was not. He was primarily a writer, authoring one of the first textbooks on cytology, and was good at reviewing and synthesizing the available research to produce a textbook. But he didn't care as much for doing the research itself, and that's where McClintock came in—she was an outstanding researcher and enjoyed the work.

Thomas Hunt Morgan

Although Barbara McClintock is known as one of the original faces of cytogenetics, she did not actually pioneer the field. That honor may belong to Thomas Hunt Morgan, who worked with fruit flies in his lab (a.k.a. the Fly Room) at Columbia University—in particular,

Thomas Hunt Morgan, a fellow pioneer in the field of cytogenetics, whose work preceded McClintock's

between 1910 and 1916. It was then that the field of cytogenetics was truly launched. In general, Morgan was *not* a follower of Mendel's theories of genetics—in his earliest works, he was actually critical of Mendelian genetics. He was also an anti-Darwinist, arguing against several of Darwin's theories.

Morgan's work with *Drosophila melanogaster* proved that genes, which are present on chromosomes, are responsible for heredity. His work inspired many geneticists who came after him to use *Drosophila* as their research organism of choice. *Drosophila* had a short reproduction cycle, obvious observable traits (particularly in eye color and wing shape), and identifiable (although very small) chromosomes that could be studied, all of which made it an obvious choice as a study organism.

Based on his groundbreaking work in the field. Morgan went on to publish twenty-two books and more than 350 scientific articles. In 1933, he won the Nobel Prize in Physiology or Medicine for his work on chromosomes and heredity.

During McClintock's tenure at Cornell and beyond, Morgan was on the faculty at the California Institute of Technology in Pasadena. But he was aware of McClintock's work and in fact helped her and Harriet Creighton publish their seminal 1931 paper on chromosomal crossover. Morgan was visiting Cornell in the spring of 1931, and Creighton shared with him the research she and McClintock had been doing on chromosomal crossover in maize. The two women had intended to wait another growing season before publishing their findings, so they would have another season's worth of data to prove their theory, but Morgan intervened and insisted that they publish immediately, on the grounds that they already had enough supporting data. He immediately wrote to the editor of the *Proceedings of the National Academy of Sciences* and informed them that Creighton and McClintock would be submitting their paper forthwith.

It later emerged that another geneticist, Curt Stern, was doing similar work with *Drosophila* and intended to present similar findings shortly. By encouraging Creighton and McClintock to publish when they did, Morgan essentially helped them "scoop" Stern, who was not pleased. Such was the drama in the cutthroat world of scientific research!

Harriet Creighton

One of McClintock's contemporaries—and her collaborator on that 1931 paper—was a young graduate student who McClintock took under her wing: Harriet Creighton. When Creighton arrived at Cornell in 1929, at the tender age of twenty, she was meant to be a teaching assistant to a paleobotanist named Dr. Petrie. However, she met Barbara McClintock on her first day there, and McClintock asked about her plan of study and steered her toward cytology and genetics. She also adopted Creighton as her research assistant.

Creighton and McClintock worked well together. Creighton quickly learned that when McClintock would make a statement that didn't seem to follow the conversation at hand, it was often a response to a question that McClintock thought Creighton *should* be asking—and thus Creighton learned to carefully consider those responses and learn from them. Creighton said of her mentor, "She was very quick to see things, and someone who wasn't quick had a hard time." Luckily for Creighton, she was a quick study.

Together, Creighton and McClintock published a landmark 1931 paper in which they proved the existence of a long-held theory: chromosomal crossover. Thomas Hunt Morgan was among the earlier scientists who had supported this theory, but until Creighton

Harriet Creighton, circa 1966

Barbara McClintock: Cytogeneticist and Discoverer of Mobile Genetic Elements

and McClintock's research and publication of their 1931 paper, it was not proven.

Marcus Rhoades

There was a Golden Age of maize cytogenetics at Cornell that lasted from about 1928 to 1935. McClintock and Creighton were among the luminaries of that age, and so was a young graduate student named Marcus Rhoades.

When Rhoades arrived at Cornell, McClintock was a newly minted PhD working on researching linkage groups and chromosomes in maize. McClintock was somewhat isolated during this period because she was attempting to handle two sides of genetic research—both the breeding of the maize crops and the chromosomal research—a task that seemed confusing and insurmountable to her contemporaries in the lab. But when Rhoades came to Cornell, intent on working with maize, he grew excited when he learned of McClintock's work and took it upon himself to explain to the other scientists the importance of McClintock's research. He became more than just a colleague to McClintock—he was also her biggest supporter and a close friend. Said McClintock to biographer Evelyn Fox Keller, "He *understood* what I was trying to do when others did not." In return for his support and companionship, McClintock gave Rhoades access to the field of maize cytogenetics.

Although Rhoades didn't win a Nobel Prize or achieve the sort of acclaim that Thomas Hunt Morgan and Barbara McClintock did, his contributions to the field of genetics should not be undervalued. Rhoades did extensive research into unstable mutations in maize, and in fact, he did pioneering work on transposition in the 1930s, years before McClintock would publish her findings about transposition and activators and dissociators. Predecessors had believed that

In 1929, the dream team at Cornell included (left to right) *Charles Burnham, Marcus Rhoades, Rollins Emerson, Barbara McClintock, and George Beadle* (kneeling in front).

genetic mutations were simply occurrences unrelated to anything in the actual cell, but Rhoades's research in the late 1930s pointed to a gene destabilizing a mutation—in other words, a gene within the cell having some control over the mutation, much like what McClintock's research later showed as well.

Rhoades's work was integral to McClintock's discovery of transposition. According to Nina Fedoroff, a molecular biologist who worked with McClintock at the Carnegie Institution after McClintock's official retirement and who authored the book *The Dynamic Genome: Barbara McClintock's Ideas in the Century of Genetics*, "Rhoades ... set the stage for McClintock. Rhoades's observation that a second gene was required for instability was very much in McClintock's awareness and important to her growing understanding of transposition."

This may look like a case of McClintock stealing Rhoades's work, but it was decidedly not. McClintock and Rhoades were close friends and colleagues who frequently shared their research and ideas. Both knew what the other was working on, and their work often overlapped. In this case, Rhoades simply did the early work that paved the way for McClintock's later research and discovery.

It was Rhoades who McClintock turned to when she left the University of Missouri and found herself well into her leave of absence with no particular place to turn. He had just taken a new position at Columbia University, and McClintock wondered where he'd be farming his maize—even in 1941, Columbia was in the middle of the urban jungle of New York City, obviously no place to grow maize. Rhoades told McClintock of his plan to farm at Cold Spring Harbor, and McClintock decided to join him.

Rollins Emerson

Backtracking just a bit, part of the reason that dream team at Cornell existed is because of Rollins A. Emerson. Emerson had rediscovered Mendelian genetics in the late 1800s, when he was performing his own experiments on beans at the University of Nebraska. While in Nebraska, he became interested in maize—which is not overly surprising, given that Nebraska, the Cornhusker State, grows a huge amount of corn. These days, it is the third-largest producer of corn in the United States, and it has long been known for its corn production. Needless to say, maize was widely available in Nebraska.

In 1914, Emerson took a position at Cornell University, establishing himself as a professor of plant breeding. He was also the head of the department of plant breeding, where McClintock, Creighton, and Rhoades all worked, along with George Beadle, who was also part of the dream team. Emerson was the common link that drew both Rhoades and Beadle to the university: he was a highly esteemed maize geneticist and known for hosting a lab that valued hard work, enthusiasm, and openness.

Notably, Emerson was among the first to suggest that mutations were responsible for the variations in organisms such as maize. Later work in cytogenetics, including McClintock's and Rhoades's, focused heavily on mutations, so certainly Emerson's early work was important to their developing interests.

George Beadle

Although Rollins Emerson had grown up in the Cornhusker State, he wasn't born there. But George Beadle was, which may explain his interest in maize cytogenetics.

Beadle was another member of the dream team at Cornell during the Golden Age of maize research. He arrived at Cornell to work with Rollins Emerson and Lester Sharp on maize genetics, fresh from the University of Nebraska.

Much like McClintock, Beadle was given the opportunity to work under a National Research Council Fellowship. He chose to work on both maize and *Drosophila*, crossing over in the two main areas of

George Beadle played a crucial role in McClintock's scientific career.

genetic research at the time. In the 1930s, Beadle went on to work on the fungus *Neurospora* as well, and it was *Neurospora* that led him to summon McClintock to Stanford University in 1944. A few years earlier, Beadle and colleagues Edward Tatum and Norman Horowitz had coined a one gene–one enzyme hypothesis that suggested that each gene produces a single enzyme that affects one step in the metabolic pathway. This hypothesis was based on his work with *Neurospora* and led to the eventual development of the field of molecular biology. But in 1944, Beadle had run into a wall because he couldn't determine the cytology of *Neurospora*—the chromosomes were too small for him to identify under a microscope.

Beadle knew that McClintock had pioneered a slide method years earlier that had allowed maize geneticists to study the cytology of maize, and he suspected she could be of help. Indeed she was. McClintock arrived at Stanford in the fall of 1944 and began to puzzle out Beadle's problem. In the first three days, she made no progress and began to be frustrated. McClintock recalled, "I was really quite petrified that maybe I was taking on more than I could really do … I realized that there was something wrong—something quite seriously wrong. I wasn't seeing things, I wasn't integrating, I wasn't getting things right at all. I was lost." This was uncharacteristic for McClintock, who had an incredibly keen eye for the inner workings of cells.

Frustrated, McClintock decided to take a walk. She sat for thirty minutes under a row of eucalyptus trees on the Stanford campus and thought and cried, uncharacteristically. She was overwhelmed, but then suddenly, the answer came to her, and she rushed back to the lab, knowing that everything was going to be resolved. McClintock said, "Suddenly … I couldn't wait to get back to the laboratory. I knew I was going to solve it—everything was going to be all right."

Within five days, the mystery was solved. McClintock counted seven chromosomes on *Neurospora* and she went a step further and tracked the individual chromosomes all the way through meiosis and mapped that process, which had until that point been unknown in fungi.

McClintock credits her time under the eucalyptus as allowing her to reset her brain to be able to see what had before only looked like chaos in the cells. "I found that the more I worked with them ... I was part of the system. I was right down there with them ... I even was able to see the internal parts of the chromosomes ... I actually felt as if I were right down there and these were my friends."

Beadle gave McClintock credit for her work, saying that in two months she "did more to clean up the cytology of *Neurospora* than all other cytological geneticists had done in all previous time on all forms of mold."

Like McClintock, Beadle was a member of the National Academy of Sciences, and also like McClintock, Beadle won the Nobel Prize in Physiology or Medicine. His honor, though, came in 1958, when he shared the prize with Edward Tatum for their work showing that genes regulate chemical events. (Beadle and Tatum shared the honor with Joshua Lederberg, who also won a prize that year for his work on genetic recombination in bacteria. Lederberg won a prize independently, and Beadle and Tatum shared a prize.)

Like Marcus Rhoades, Beadle was more than just a colleague of Barbara McClintock. He was also a close friend and a staunch supporter.

Lewis Stadler

Another colleague who became a close friend of Barbara McClintock's was Lewis Stadler. The two met at Cornell when Stadler was there on a

National Research Council Fellowship to work with Rollins Emerson. Both Stadler and McClintock were interested in maize genetics.

McClintock found herself fascinated by Stadler's research into the effects of X-rays on maize. Stadler was studying the mutations that occurred in maize due to X-rays, and McClintock eagerly agreed to help on Stadler's research in 1931. Of the time she spent working with Stadler that summer, McClintock said, "That was a profitable summer for me! I was very excited about what I was seeing, because many of these were new things. It was also helping to place different genes on different chromosomes—it was a very fast way to do it." (Normally occurring mutations can take generations to appear, but by exposing the maize to radiation, scientists could speed up the rate of mutation.) In fact, it was McClintock's work with Stadler that led her to develop her theory of ring chromosomes.

Stadler was a huge supporter of McClintock. When she realized the time had come to leave Cornell, he was instrumental in helping her secure a position in 1936, despite the country being in the throes of the Great Depression. Stadler was on the faculty of the University of Missouri, and he essentially created an assistant professor position for McClintock, as he was eager to have her on board for the new genetic research center he was building at the university. McClintock stayed at the university for five years, but ultimately it was not a good fit for her. The dean and other faculty did not hold her in the same regard as Stadler did, and she was told that if Stadler were to leave the university, her position would end, too. (The university later tried to lure her back when she secured a prestigious nomination to the National Academy of Sciences, but they were unsuccessful.)

THE 1950S FALLOUT

The biggest detractors of Barbara McClintock's work came after she attempted to present her theories of transposition, beginning at the 1951 Cold Spring Harbor Symposium, where her speech was met with cold stares and confusion. McClintock's work had generally been well regarded for more than two decades, and the frosty reception she got at the symposium or when she tried to explain her work afterwards confused her. "It was a surprise that I was being ridiculed, or being told that I was really mad," she said. Fellow scientists thought her idea was crazy, and one prominent geneticist even referred to her as "just an old bag who'd been hanging around Cold Spring Harbor for years."

McClintock continued her research and tried on repeated occasions to present the information again to explain her theories. But time and again she was met with confusion or outright hostility. The theory of transposition was simply too complex and too radical for most geneticists of the time to accept.

McClintock got the last laugh, though, when she scored the Nobel Prize in 1983. She was far too gracious to note it, but a small part of her must have been pleased that her supposed craziness was finally recognized as the intelligent, well-researched theory that it actually was.

Stadler's research into the mutagenic effects of X-rays was well known and gained him a strong reputation, but his life and career were cut rather short when he died of leukemia at the age of fifty-seven.

Milislav Demerec

When Barbara McClintock made the decision to leave the University of Missouri, she was unsure of where to go next. Ultimately, she called her friend and former colleague Marcus Rhoades, who told her of his plan to farm at Cold Spring Harbor. McClintock had a connection at Cold Spring Harbor—a geneticist she had known for years named Milislav Demerec. Demerec worked on *Drosophila*, and he knew McClintock and was highly supportive of her research in maize genetics.

Demerec immediately invited McClintock to come out to Cold Spring Harbor for the summer. She did, and when winter hit and she had gone back to New York to stay in Marcus Rhoades's extra room, it wasn't long at all before she received a call from Demerec, offering her a job at Cold Spring Harbor. Demerec had become the director of the department of genetics for the Carnegie Insitution at Cold Spring Harbor, and he immediately knew he wanted McClintock on board.

McClintock was not quite so sure. She hadn't decided whether she wanted to settle there, but at Demerec's urging, she met with Vannevar Bush, the president of the Carnegie Institution, and the two had such a positive meeting that she ended up accepting the appointment. It was a wise move—she had a place to grow her corn, a lab to do her research, a home to sleep in, a salary, and as she would later learn, a place to spend the rest of her life.

Demerec was another protégé of Rollins Emerson at Cornell, which was his initial connection to McClintock. He initially worked on maize genetics as a doctoral student at Cornell, but he later switched his focus to *Drosophila virilis*. Still later, he changed focus again and began to research bacterial genetics and antibiotic resistance. Like McClintock, Rhoades, and Beadle, he was a member of the prestigious National Academy of Sciences.

DETRACTORS

Barbara McClintock had numerous contemporaries and colleagues who admired and respected her work, and many of them became her friends. But no one is wholly without adversaries, and certainly McClintock had a couple.

One of her earliest was Curt Stern, a German-born geneticist who worked with *Drosophila*. At the same time as McClintock and Creighton were proving their theory of chromosomal crossover in maize, Stern was working on similar research on *Drosophila*. McClintock and Creighton beat him to the press with their publication of their findings thanks to the intervention of Thomas Hunt Morgan, and Stern was reportedly none too pleased. He had presented his findings publicly, and a colleague from the Kaiser Wilhelm Institute in Germany then approached him and said that Creighton and McClintock had just published essentially the same findings that Stern had just declared unique. Stern, who had been feeling triumphant about the success of his presentation, said, "I am still grateful to my colleague for permitting me the feeling of triumph for half an hour longer than I would have had it if he had told me about the Creighton-McClintock paper *before* my talk."

Naturally, Stern wasn't thrilled to be scooped, but it also didn't seem to cause any long-term animosity between the scientists. When McClintock received a Guggenheim Fellowship to research in Germany in 1933, for example, her intention was to go work with Curt Stern. That didn't end up happening because Stern, a Jew, had fled to the United States to avoid the reign of Hitler.

Instead, McClintock came to Germany and worked with Richard Goldschmidt, Stern's colleague at the Kaiser Wilhelm Institute. McClintock's time in Germany lasted just over four months. At that point she returned to the United States, horrified at what she had seen in Hitler's Germany. But for a short time, she did indeed work with Goldschmidt, who was a rather controversial figure at times.

Goldschmidt was generally held in high esteem for his genetics work, but he was openly critical of contemporary genetic theory—particularly those from the Thomas Hunt Morgan school of thought. At a time when interests were beginning to move toward molecular studies, Goldschmidt remained focused on cytogenetics—as did McClintock, although she was not as outspoken as Goldschmidt was. Nevertheless, the two shared a common bond over their concerns about the shift in genetic theory.

However, their schools of thought diverged in other areas. Goldschmidt was an outspoken critic of chromosomal-Mendelian genetics, whereas McClintock fell in the camp of chromosomal-Mendelian genetics. Furthermore, Goldschmidt had a tendency to posit theories without much evidence behind them, whereas McClintock felt it essential to back up any and all theories without copious evidence.

Overall, McClintock tended to agree with many of Goldschmidt's theories, but she most assuredly did *not* agree with how he presented them.

Interestingly, McClintock was decidedly quiet about her beliefs compared to Goldschmidt's outspoken, critical nature, and yet she was still considered too much of a troublemaker for one of her main critics—W. C. Curtis, the dean of liberal arts at the University of

Missouri. McClintock was not well liked by her colleagues at the university—the generally conservative group felt she was a maverick and not a suitable addition to the faculty. And so, in 1940 Curtis decided not to keep McClintock on at the university. He expressed to the Rockefeller Foundation that he hoped she would secure another appointment so that she would leave the university.

Curtis got his wish, though not in the way he had thought. McClintock decided she'd had enough of the university and took an indefinite leave of absence from which she never returned. After that, it was on to Cold Spring Harbor and bigger and better things.

OVERALL RECEPTION IN THE FIELD

In general, over the very long span of her working years, Barbara McClintock was well regarded in her field. Her theory of transposition earned her a loss of support in the scientific community, but decades later the value of her contributions was recognized. Overall, her body of work has been solid and long-lasting—as her strongest supporters always knew it would be.

Barbara McClintock, circa 1981

CHAPTER FIVE

BARBARA MCCLINTOCK'S IMPACT ON CYTOGENETICS

arbara McClintock spent decades in semi-obscurity. Certainly, she was known within her field in the 1950s, 1960s, and early 1970s, when she was mostly working quietly in her lab, but because she wasn't really publishing or presenting during that time, she wasn't in the forefront of most of her fellow scientist's minds. To most of the general public, her name was unknown.

That changed when scientists began to rediscover her work—particularly her discoveries about transposition—and realize the importance it had on the field. By the time she won the Nobel Prize in 1983, her reputation had been restored and her contributions well recognized. Looking back at her body of work, it's clear to see the incredible impact Barbara McClintock had on the field of cytogenetics.

HER MAJOR DISCOVERIES

Barbara McClintock's breakthroughs and discoveries were numerous, but several stand out and cemented her place as a vital figure in the history of genetics.

Chromosome Identification in Maize

McClintock's first major accomplishment in the field was identifying the chromosomes in maize. Scientists already knew that maize contained ten chromosomes, but they couldn't tell much about them—they couldn't distinguish specific characteristics on each chromosome. McClintock solved that problem.

Scientist John Belling had been experimenting with dye and squashing plant cells to get a better look at their cytology, but he hadn't yet perfected it. McClintock played around with Belling's technique until she found a way to increase the clarity of the slides, by heating the slide and using acid to remove the red dye stain, which improved the contrast in the chromosomes. Now, McClintock could better see each chromosome and analyze its specific features.

She also experimented with studying cells from a different part of the maize plant than other scientists had been using. Traditionally, scientists had studied cells from the root tips of the maize; instead, McClintock looked at cells from the pollen-bearing tassel of the plant. The cells in the tassel were dividing in anticipation of reproduction, which made them ideal for scientific study.

In 1929, McClintock shared her findings from her chromosome analysis in the journal *Science*. It was a major breakthrough in maize genetics.

Chromosomal Crossover

McClintock's next major breakthrough came in 1931 when she and Harriet Creighton published a landmark paper on chromosomal crossover. Scientists already knew that the genes for so-called "linked" traits, which passed together from parent to child, were on the same

Barbara McClintock and Harriet Creighton in 1956, more than two decades after they published their landmark paper

chromosome and generally passed together. But sometimes certain expected traits were not inherited in child generations, and geneticists hadn't yet figured out why or how that occurred. They assumed it was due to some sort of crossover of chromosomes, but they had yet to prove their theory.

McClintock and Creighton solved the problem and proved the theory by focusing on a particular portion of chromosome 9 that had a knob on one end and a stretched-out tip on the other. They hand-pollinated to create a child generation of maize that would allow them to carefully track what was happening on chromosome 9, and indeed they found the proof they were expecting: evidence that the knob and stretched-out tip corresponded to certain traits in the maize (a purple color and a waxiness on the kernel) and that during meiosis pieces of the chromosome had crossed over and switched places in some cases. In short, they had proved that the exchange of chromosomal material during meiosis corresponded to the physical traits of an organism's offspring, which explained why offspring can have traits different from their parents.

So monumental was this discovery that it is considered one of the greatest experiments of modern biology.

Ring Chromosomes

In 1931, McClintock spent some time at the University of Missouri on a fellowship, working with Lewis Stadler, her friend and fellow maize geneticist. He was working on the study of radiation effects on maize chromosomes, and McClintock was fascinated by his work and eager to participate. Mutations occur naturally in any organism and were a fertile area of study for geneticists, but their occurrence was naturally slow. Using X-ray technology on maize greatly sped up the rate of mutations, giving maize geneticists more to study.

As it turned out, the partnership with Stadler led to another major discovery for McClintock. While working with him, McClintock grew interested in the broken chromosomes resulting from the radiation. She saw translocations, inversions, and deletions occurring on the chromosomes, and she also noticed that there seemed to be some missing genetic fragments that appeared to cause variations in the maize. In wondering about these missing pieces, she surmised that the ends of the fragments must be joining together to form a ring. Because of its structure, then, that ring could not participate in the cell duplication process, and thus it would get "lost."

Scientists accepted her theory because it was logical and because McClintock herself was so enthused about it. But she secretly began to doubt herself because no one had actually *seen* a ring chromosome. She was terrified that her hypothesis wouldn't turn out to be true, when her fellow scientists had already accepted it as fact.

As it happened, McClintock's gut feeling and assumption were correct. When she examined the genetic material from her test offspring maize plants, she found exactly what she had suspected: ring chromosomes. Naturally, she breathed a sigh of relief!

The Nucleolar Organizer

After her work with Lewis Stadler in Missouri, McClintock spent some time at the California Institute of Technology under her fellowship, working with Thomas Hunt Morgan and George Beadle, among others. There, she quickly made her next discovery: what she called the nucleolar organizer.

McClintock noticed a small piece of material at the end of chromosome 6, right near the cell's nucleolus, and she became curious about its function. In observing that material during the cell development process, McClintock became convinced that the material somehow organized material to create the nucleolus. "I don't know why, but I was sure it had the key," she said.

As molecular biologists would confirm decades later, McClintock's theory was correct: that piece of chromosome 6 did indeed have a role in creating the nucleolus. But the fact that she was able to deduce this in the 1930s, without the benefit of an electron microscope, is nothing short of astounding.

Perhaps not surprisingly, the theory was not particularly well received when she presented it. It was too complicated for even many scientists to understand, and without the benefit of electron microscope technology, McClintock couldn't visually show what she expected was happening. But now, decades later, her hypothesis has been verified and recognized for the breakthrough that it was.

The Breakage-Fusion-Bridge Cycle

When McClintock's fellowship funding ran out in 1935, she decided it was time to leave Cornell and pursue her work in another location. But it was the Great Depression, and research jobs were hard to come by. She turned to Lewis Stadler, who had offered her a position at the University of Missouri, and she returned there even though it wasn't exactly her dream environment.

McClintock faced a lot of opposition at the university, partly because she was a woman in a male-dominated field, but also partly because she didn't exactly conform to social niceties. At that time, women were generally expected to always be polite and accommodating despite the circumstances, and McClintock didn't hesitate to voice her displeasure when she was treated in a manner unequal to her male colleagues. It didn't exactly endear her to the male faculty, who took exception to many of her actions. At one point she reportedly got locked out of her office, so she climbed in a window. It seemed a reasonable solution to McClintock, but apparently such behavior was unacceptable from a teacher or researcher, and her fellow faculty were not pleased.

Despite the rather hostile atmosphere at the university, though, McClintock made another major breakthrough in cytological research.

Continuing on her study of broken chromosomes, she developed her theory of the breakage-fusion-bridge cycle. In this cycle, she hypothesized, broken chromosomes sometimes reanneal in an inverted fashion, which can lead them to have two centromeres instead of the usual one. During cell division, then, there is a chromatin bridge formed between the centromeres that is stressed and then breaks. The cycle repeats, sometimes many times, leading to mass genetic mutations.

Previously, scientists had believed that the rejoining of chromosomes was generally a random event, but McClintock's discovery of the breakage-fusion-bridge cycle proved that there were very specific forces at work during cell division that were ultimately responsible for the resulting genetic mutations.

A Diversion to Fungus

The vast majority of McClintock's work was done on maize, but occasionally she worked on other organisms. Most notably, in 1944 she went to Stanford University for two months at the request of her friend and former Cornell colleague George Beadle, who was now working on a form of mold called *Neurospora*.

Beadle had made significant discoveries in his work with *Neurospora*, in particular the suggestion of a one gene–one enzyme theory stating that each gene produces one enzyme that affects a single piece of the metabolic pathway. However, he was at somewhat of a standstill in his research because he couldn't determine the cytology of *Neurospora*. The chromosomes were too small for him to identify under a microscope.

At first, McClintock struggled with the task too, but after a few days and a breakthrough in her way of examining the cells, she was able to isolate and count the chromosomes on *Neurospora* and map out

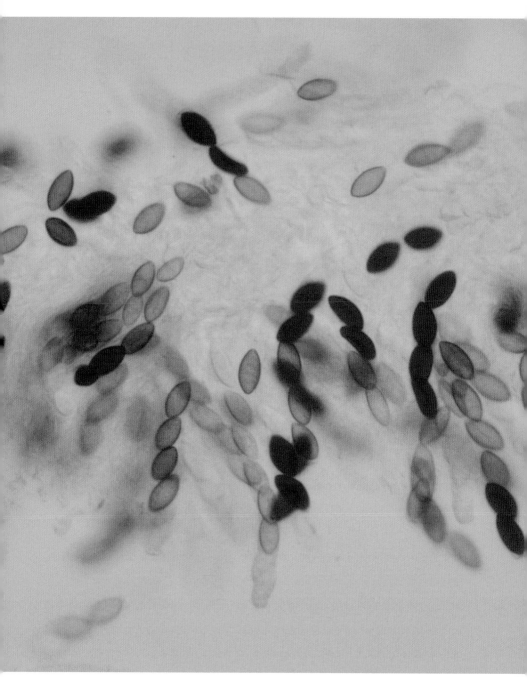

McClintock assisted fellow scientist George Beadle on his work with Neurospora, *a bread mold.*

their meiotic process, which had previously been unknown. In short, McClintock demystified the cytology of fungi in just a few short weeks.

Transposition: The Brick Wall

After leaving the University of Missouri, McClintock went to Cold Spring Harbor and ultimately accepted a research position there (with a brief diversion to Stanford to work on *Neurospora*). It was there that she made probably her biggest discovery and contribution to the field: transposition, or jumping genes.

Ironically, this groundbreaking discovery nearly torpedoed her career. It flew in the face of what scientists believed they knew about genetics, and it was such a complicated subject that few scientists could even understand it. Plus, it came at a time when molecular biology was taking off, and scientists were shifting their focus to pursue the study of bacteria and other single-celled organisms. The structure of DNA would be discovered just a couple of years later, creating a flurry of excitement in molecular biology, and McClintock's discovery of transposition would be virtually ignored.

Transposition, the discovery that turned off so much of the scientific community, was, at its most basic level, a theory that said genes could move to new sites on chromosomes. Previously, geneticists believed that the position of genes on chromosomes was fixed—they were like individual beads on a string, always in the same pattern. But McClintock's work in the 1940s revealed surprising results: The genes could move on the chromosomes, and when they did, it wasn't a random occurrence—it was controlled by an activator and a dissociator. The activator governed which gene should jump (the dissociator) and the degree to which it should. The resulting mutation, she found, was dependent on the activator's commands to the dissociator.

It's a complicated process—indeed, it was so complicated that the scientists who heard McClintock's presentation in 1951 at the Cold Spring Harbor Symposium left either confused or laughing at McClintock's "crazy" theory. Artist Nigel Holmes, while working for *Time* magazine years after McClintock's initial discovery of transposition, drew a cartoon to explain the process in simple terms.

McClintock was disheartened by the negative reaction to her theory of transposition, but she remained staunch in her belief in the process. She continued her research on mobile genetic elements and tried several times over the next years to present her hypotheses again. Each time, she was met with opposition or disinterest. That didn't change for more than two decades, until advances in molecular biology led scientists to see the likelihood that her early theory of transposition was indeed true.

Eventually, of course, scientists *did* realize the impact of her theory of transposition, and she received the prestigious Nobel Prize. It was a long time coming, but McClintock never wavered in her belief that genes were, in fact, mobile elements.

PUBLICATIONS AND PRESENTATIONS

Barbara McClintock largely stopped publishing her work in the 1950s. She still contributed to the annual reports for the Carnegie Institution, but she stopped submitting her work to scientific journals after she received such a dismal reception to her work on transposition. Researchers and academics often live and die by publishing—there's a saying in academia that you must "publish or perish." So McClintock's decision *not* to publish was unusual. But the truth was, she just didn't particularly care. It was clear that the scientific community was uninterested or downright discouraging about her latest work, and

Genes control the colors of a kernel. The Structural Gene (SG) will make the kernel dark unless disrupted.

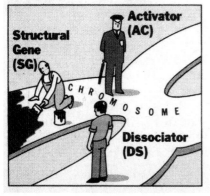

Structural Gene (SG)

Activator (AC)

CHROMOSOME

Dissociator (DS)

Disruption occurs if the Activator (AC) summons the Dissociator (DS) from another chromosome location. DS may "jump" to SG and suppress the coloring of the kernel.

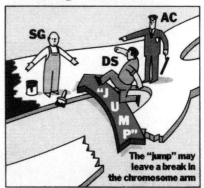

SG

DS

AC

"JUMP"

The "jump" may leave a break in the chromosome arm

If again summoned by AC, DS may move away from SG, who goes back to the coloring work. A speckled kernel results from this sequence.

SG

DS

AC

But if DS maintains its influence on SG without interruption from AC, the kernel will be entirely uncolored.

SG

DS

AC

CHROMOSOME

TIME Diagram by Nigel Holmes

Nigel Holmes's representation of transposition, published in Time *magazine.*

McClintock was perfectly happy to do her research *without* input from a community that didn't support her. The Carnegie Institution didn't push her to publish, so she didn't.

In fact, the Carnegie Institution was incredibly supportive of her work. McClintock said of the institution, "I don't think there could be a finer institution for allowing you to do what you want to do. Now if I had been at some other place I'm sure that I would have been fired for what I was doing, because nobody was accepting it. The Carnegie Institution never once told me that I shouldn't be doing it. They never once said I should publish when I wasn't publishing … [They] just let me do what I wanted and supported me all the way along the line."

Still, McClintock managed to author an impressive number of articles over the years. Including her reports for the Carnegie Institution, she wrote or contributed to more than seventy publications. She was particularly prolific in her years at Cornell, authoring or coauthoring sixteen publications. One of the best known was 1931's "A Correlation of Cytological and Genetical Crossing-Over in *Zea mays*," which she coauthored with Harriet Creighton.

Also well known were 1950's "The Original and Behavior of Mutable Loci in Maize" and 1953's "Induction of Instability at Selected Loci in Maize," both of which concerned transposition and were not well received at the time, though they are now recognized to be seminal works. The same is true with her 1934 publication "The Relation of a Particular Chromosomal Element to the Development of the Nucleoli in *Zea mays*." The stark reality was that the concepts in McClintock's publications were often simply too complicated to be understood at the time they were originally presented.

Similarly, McClintock largely stopped presenting her work in the 1950s, after the cold reception to her work on transposition. She presented a few more times in an effort to further educate people on transposition, but she was met with similarly cool responses. From then on, she simply went about her research for decades, until the accolades began.

AWARDS AND ACCOLADES

The majority of Barbara McClintock's awards and accolades came in the 1970s and 1980s, after scientists realized the true value of her contributions to the field. Still, she did receive some acclaim earlier in her career. She was awarded with fellowships from the National Research Council, the Guggenheim Foundation, and the Rockefeller Foundation in the 1930s—all prestigious fellowships to earn. In 1939, she was elected vice-president of the Genetics Society of America. She went on to be elected their first woman president in 1945, a notable honor indeed.

In 1944, McClintock earned a prestigious election to the National Academy of Sciences, and in 1946, she was elected to the American Philosophical Society as well. In 1947, the American Association of University Women awarded her an Achievement Award. Twelve years later, she was made a member of the American Academy of Arts and Sciences. In 1965, she was appointed Andrew D. White Professor-at-Large at Cornell, an honor given to "outstanding intellectuals" at Cornell. And in 1967, she won the Kimber Genetics Award from the National Academy of Sciences, given "for distinguished achievement in the broad field of genetics," as well as a Distinguished Service Award from the Carnegie Institution; she remained a Distinguished Service Member until her death in 1992. In 1970, she became the first woman to win the National Medal of Science, which she was awarded by President Richard Nixon. This distinguished honor, bestowed by the National Science

King Carl Gustaf of Sweden presented McClintock with the Nobel Prize in 1983.

The ultimate feather in any scientist's cap is a Nobel Prize. For Barbara McClintock, the prestigious honor was a long time coming—more than three decades, in fact. In 1983, she received the Nobel Prize in Physiology or Medicine for her pioneering work on mobile genetic elements (or "jumping genes"), which she had tried unsuccessfully to share in the 1950s.

Notably, McClintock was the first woman to receive an unshared Nobel Prize in that particular category—and she was only the third woman in history to win an unshared Nobel Prize in any science category. Notoriously shy from public events and accolades, McClintock was actually quite pleased to be able to walk to the stage to receive her prize on the arm of King Carl Gustaf of Sweden.

Finally, McClintock got the recognition she had been denied decades earlier. The audience present at the awards ceremony reportedly applauded so loud that the floor shook when McClintock took the stage. Although McClintock had said, "You don't need the public recognition … You just need the respect of your colleagues," it was no doubt a relief to no longer be mocked or ignored for her ideas.

She did, however, have to deal with the recognition that came from having won the prestigious award. After the ceremony, she longed to return to her quiet days in the lab, but instead she was the subject of much interest from the scientific community and the media. Although she appreciated the honor, McClintock said, "I don't like publicity. I don't like my time taken up with me … At my age, it's quite a chore." Such is the life of a Nobel Prize winner.

Foundation, was established to honor scientists "deserving of special recognition by reason of their outstanding contributions to knowledge in the physical, biological, mathematical, or engineering sciences."

In the late 1970s, her work was beginning to be recognized for the groundbreaking achievement that it was, and the awards began to roll in more steadily. In 1978 she won both the Louis and Bert Freedman Foundation Award and the Lewis S. Rosenstiel Award for Distinguished Work in Basic Medical Research from Brandeis University.

In 1980, the Genetics Society of America saluted her. And 1981 was a big year in which she won the inaugural MacArthur Prize Fellow Laureate Award (a lifetime award that offered her a yearly monetary award); the Albert Lasker Award for Basic Medical Research; the Wolf Prize in Medicine; and, with Marcus Rhoades, the first Thomas Hunt Morgan Medal from the Genetics Society of America. The latter prize was quite an honor, as it recognizes "lifetime achievement in the field of genetics." Finally, McClintock's entire body of work was being honored!

In 1982, she claimed the Louisa Gross Horwitz Prize for Biology or Biochemistry from Columbia University. Then in 1983, there was that little thing called the Nobel Prize.

Over the years, McClintock was bestowed with fifteen honorary doctoral degrees. She was inducted into the National Women's Hall of Fame three years after receiving the Nobel Prize. She even had a commemorative stamp from the US Postal Service issued in her likeness, in the American Scientists series.

Perhaps closest to home, Cold Spring Harbor, her home for the last few decades of her career, named the McClintock Laboratory after her in 1973. And in 1989, the Carnegie Institution established in her honor the Barbara McClintock Fellowship Fund, which awards two-year fellowships for postdoctoral students at the institution.

IMPACT ON THE CYTOGENETICS OF TODAY

There is no doubt that McClintock's work had a massive impact on cytogenetics today. Her longtime friend and colleague Marcus Rhoades said in 1969 that "genetics would not occupy its present high estate were it not for her magnificent and pioneering contributions."

Her contributions continue to inform genetics today. Presently, genetics is a huge field of study as scientists learn more about genetically inherited disease and chromosomal anomalies such as Down syndrome and microdeletions. Her pioneering work in mobile genetic elements, in fact, has helped inform the study that geneticists do today on understanding what happens to minute pieces of genetic information that break off of chromosomes and sometimes reattach in other locations. As Dr. Maxine Singer, former president of the Carnegie Institution noted, "Now there is a lively international field of research on [transposable elements]. We have come to appreciate that they play an important role in the evolution of genomes." Indeed, extensive research into chromosomal disorders is being done by such organizations as Unique, based out of the United Kingdom, as scientists work to unravel the complex code that leads to genetic anomalies and mutations. Without McClintock's research into transposition and mobile genetic elements, this type of research likely would not be possible.

Genetic research in current times is somewhat of a double-edged sword. On one hand, it has provided scientists with far more insight into many chromosomal anomalies and genetic disorders than was available in the past. The most common chromosomal disorder, Down syndrome, was not largely understood until scientist Jerome Lejeune studied the chromosomal makeup of individuals with the syndrome and learned

ANOTHER GENETICS GIANT: MARY-CLAIRE KING

Although Barbara McClintock focused her studies on cytogenetics, when molecular biology became a prominent scientific field, many geneticists chose to focus on that side of genetics—studying bacteria and the genetic side of diseases and conditions. Still, the work McClintock did on demystifying chromosomes and mobile genes informed their later work on the molecular end of things.

One such prominent geneticist is another female in the field: Mary-Claire King. Born in 1946, she currently teaches at the University of Washington. One of King's many achievements is in fact related to the BRCA gene. In 1990, King isolated a gene on chromosome 17 and determined that it is responsible for hereditary cases of breast and ovarian cancer. Not all breast cancers are hereditary—current statistics estimate that up to one-tenth are, though. And for those cancers, the BRCA1 gene that King isolated is a cause. King also identified a second gene, BRCA2, located on chromosome 13, that is a cause of breast cancer.

Much like scientists initially shunned McClintock's theory of transposition, scientists initially disbelieved King's theory that genetics was a factor in certain human diseases. Her discovery of BRCA1 and BRCA2 changed that.

Like McClintock, King is not a one-trick pony. She has also made research advancements on the genetic components of other diseases and conditions such as certain autoimmune diseases and inherited deafness. And her early groundbreaking work was in proving that humans and chimpanzees are 99 percent genetically identical.

Like McClintock, Mary-Claire King found her theories were not always immediately accepted among the scientific community.

that they had three copies of chromosome 21. (In most cases—there is actually a rare form of Down syndrome known as translocation that falls along the lines of McClintock's theory of transposition—a piece of chromosome 21 breaks off and reattaches itself to another chromosome, usually chromosome 14.) Knowing that the extra chromosome causes Down syndrome has allowed researchers to make tremendous progress in learning how Down syndrome affects individuals and how certain conditions that go along with it can be treated. And, in fact, scientists have recently found that the extra genetic material associated with

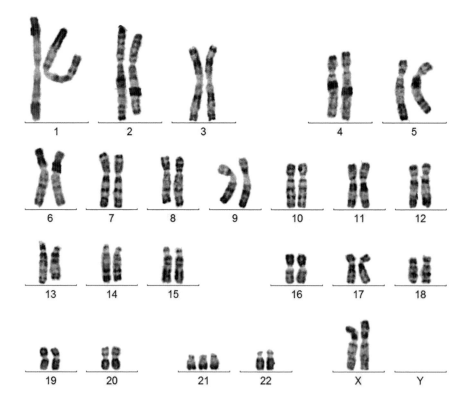

A karyotype shows the presence of an extra twenty-first chromosome.

chromosome 21 is providing them with insights into Alzheimer's research—promising studies and drug trials are being conducted based on this knowledge, which never would've been possible if it were not for the work of early cytogeneticists such as Barbara McClintock.

But along with the positives that come with genetic research, there are potential darker sides. Scientists have now discovered ways to test for chromosomal abnormalities in a fetus while a woman is pregnant, and that information can be used to decide to terminate the fetus's life or to make medical decisions that have potential life-and-death consequences with regard to the fetus.

Prenatal testing for genetic issues is a minefield, with some arguing that knowledge is power, and it is useful to know the genetic makeup of a child before it's born, and others arguing that this knowledge leads to a slippery slope of "designer babies" and eugenics—that is, parents can use the knowledge of their child's genetic makeup to decide whether to consider a pregnancy. This then leads to sticky moral questions about the value of a life: How do parents and the medical community decide which genetic profiles constitute a valuable life and which do not?

Further, genetic research also leads into a minefield of medical care and insurance questions. When an individual's genetic code is known, if there is anything abnormal or unusual in it, in some instances that can be used to deny proper health care or insurance.

Along with the sticky moral issues also come positive applications. If a fetus is known to have certain anomalies in utero, they can sometimes be addressed before the baby is born, improving potential health outcomes. Currently, for example, there is testing underway on treatments that could potentially lessen the cognitive impairment of individuals with Down syndrome if they are applied when a fetus is under ten weeks of development in utero. Naturally, to apply such a treatment, one would have to know that the fetus did indeed have Down syndrome—so there is a case where early detection of a chromosomal issue could be a positive.

Scientists have now found genes definitively linked to certain types of breast and colon cancer, for example. If an individual undergoes genetic testing and determines he or she carries one of these genes, proactive measures can be taken to significantly lower the risk of cancer from developing. Actress and filmmaker Angelina Jolie is perhaps the most famous face of this: based on her mother's health history, she underwent genetic testing and found she had mutations of the BRCA genes, which are known to be a strong factor in breast and ovarian cancer. Jolie subsequently opted for a preventative mastectomy and hysterectomy to avoid the very strong possibility of developing cancer.

So, like anything, cytogenetic knowledge has its positives and its negatives. Barbara McClintock and others gave us the science; it's up to us what we do with the ethics and moral obligations related to that science.

LOOKING AHEAD

Back when Barbara McClintock was entering the field, the path wasn't smooth for women. She had plenty of supporters to help her along the way, but she also faced her share of discriminatory practices, based on her gender and the fact that she didn't conform to expected gender norms.

Although there is still a disparity in pay grades between women and men in some industries and fields, the fact is that in our current society, women have opportunities that didn't exist even a few decades ago. But women are still the minority in the sciences. According to the US Census Bureau, women in STEM (science, technology, engineering,

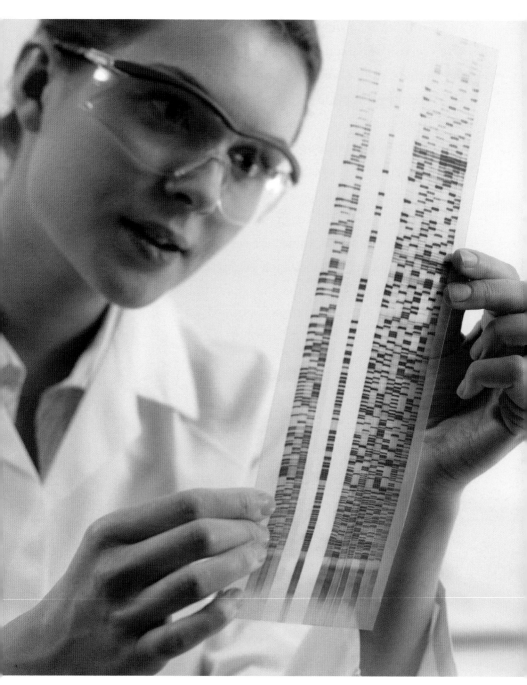

Today, women are still underrepresented in STEM fields.

and math) fields constitute only 26 percent of the science workforce. That's certainly an improvement over the 7 percent that they made up in 1970, but it's still a minority. The reasons for this range from gender bias to family planning to sexual harassment to simply upbringing— parents may, consciously or unconsciously, steer female children to more traditionally female occupations.

However, there is a big push to get more women into the STEM fields, and certainly the opportunities are there for women who are interested in the field. Thanks to pioneers like Barbara McClintock, it's certainly evident that women are every bit as capable of scientific inquiry and discovery as their male counterparts.

The field is wide open and the opportunities are there, for the women who want to pursue them.

CHRONOLOGY

1902   Born on June 16, 1902.

1919   Enrolls at Cornell University.

1923   Graduates Cornell with a degree in botany.

1925   Earns master's degree at Cornell.

1927   Earns doctoral degree at Cornell.

1931   Publishes landmark paper on chromosomal crossover with Harriet Creighton.

1931–1936   Researches at Cornell, University of Missouri, California Institute of Technology, and in Germany under fellowships from National Research Council, Guggenheim Foundation, and Rockefeller Foundation. Discovers ring chromosomes, nucleolar organizer, and breakage-fusion-bridge cycle.

1936–1941   Works in teaching and research at University of Missouri.

1939   Becomes vice-president of the Genetics Society of America.

1941   Joins Carnegie Institution at Cold Spring Harbor Laboratory as a researcher, where she remains for the rest of her working life.

1944	Goes to Stanford and works on cytology of *Neurospora*. Receives election to the National Academy of Sciences. Begins research on mobile genetic elements, or "jumping genes."
1945	Elected president of the Genetics Society of America, the first woman to hold the title.
1951	Presents paper about mobile genetic elements at Cold Spring Harbor Symposium. Receives unfavorable response.
1953	Presents again about mobile genetic elements and receives a similar response. Meanwhile, James Watson and Francis Crick present their landmark findings on the structure of DNA, which shifts scientific focus to molecular biology.
1956	Presents yet again about mobile genetic elements, and receives yet another unfavorable response.
1963–1969	Works with geneticists in Central and South America on maize genetics.
1970	Receives the National Medal of Science, the first woman to achieve the honor.
1973	McClintock Laboratory dedicated at Cold Spring Harbor.

1981	Becomes first recipient of the MacArthur Prize Fellow Laureate Award. Also receives the Albert Lasker Award, the Wolfe Prize in Medicine, and the first Thomas Hunt Morgan Medal (with Marcus Rhoades).
1983	Becomes the first woman to win an unshared Nobel Prize in Physiology or Medicine.
1992	Dies in Huntington, New York.

GLOSSARY

affirmative action A policy that favors people from a historically disadvantaged group.

American Dream A philosophy that all citizens can achieve success using hard work and initiative.

chromatin The materials that make up all organisms other than bacteria.

chromomere A bead-shaped mass of chromatin that is arranged in a linear sequence.

chromosomal crossover The exchange of genetic material by chromosomes involved in meiosis.

chromosome A thread-like structure that contains genetic material and is found in the nucleus of most cells.

crossbreed To breed two different species.

cytogenetics The study of heredity as it relates to chromosomes.

cytology The study of plant and animal cells.

DNA Acronym for deoxyribonucleic acid; the carrier of genetic material. Its form is a double-helix structure, and it is the main constituent of chromosomes.

doctoral Related to a doctorate-level degree.

dominant traits A trait that will appear in an offspring if at least one parent contributes it. Dominant traits will generally override recessive traits.

Down syndrome A congenital syndrome that occurs when an individual has three copies of chromosome 21 instead of the usual two. People with Down syndrome typically have intellectual disabilities and sometimes physical disabilities, as well as distinctive physical features.

Dust Bowl An area made up of territory in Oklahoma, Kansas, and Texas that experienced severe soil erosion in the early 1930s. Many farmers had to leave the region because of it.

flapper Essentially, a "party girl" of the 1920s. Flappers typically dressed in a particular type of dress and wore a distinctive bobbed hairstyle.

gene A unit of heredity that is found on a chromosome and generally passes from parent to offspring.

genotype An organism's genetic makeup.

glass ceiling A barrier to advancement in a professional field. Usually applies to women and/or minorities.

GMO Genetically modified organism; an organism that has been purposely genetically modified.

Great Depression An economic slump that began with the stock market crash in 1929 and lasted throughout most of the 1930s.

heredity The passing on of traits from one generation to the next.

indigenous Native to a particular place.

maize Corn.

meiosis A form of cell division where a cell divides twice to produce four offspring cells.

molecular biology A subset of the science of biology that deals with macromolecules such as proteins and nucleic acids.

nucleolus A small structure present in the nucleus of a cell.

phenotype An organism's observable traits that arise from that organism's genotype.

PKU Phenylketonuria, an inherited disorder that can cause brain and nerve damage.

prophylactic Meant to prevent disease.

Punnett square A diagram to help determine inheritance outcomes in crossbreeding.

reanneal Rejoin.

recessive traits Traits that may be carried in a person's genotype but not apparent in the person. A dominant trait will override a recessive trait, so the recessive trait may not be visible in a person.

ring chromosome A broken chromosome whose ends have fused together.

space race The competition between the United States and the Soviet Union during the Cold War to see which would achieve more in space exploration.

tenure Guaranteed permanent employment in the teaching field.

translocation The movement of one part of a chromosome to another location on the chromosome or on a different chromosome.

transposition The act of moving something from one area to another.

FURTHER INFORMATION

BOOKS

Comfort, Nathaniel C. *The Tangled Field: Barbara McClintock's Search for the Patterns of Genetic Control.* Boston: Harvard University Press, 2003.

Fine, Edith Hope. *Barbara McClintock: Nobel Prize Geneticist.* San Diego: eFrog Press, 2012.

Keller, Evelyn Fox. *A Feeling for the Organism: The Life and Work of Barbara McClintock.* New York: Henry Holt, 1983.

WEBSITES

Genetics
http://www.genetics.org
This is the official website for the scientific journal *Genetics*.

Genetics Home Reference
http://ghr.nlm.nih.gov
This website created by the US National Library of Medicine provides user-friendly information about genetics.

Understanding Genetics
http://genetics.thetech.org
This website contains videos, books, and online exhibits related to genetics, as well as an Ask a Geneticist section.

VIDEOS

Barbara McClintock Tribute Film

http://www.youtube.com/watch?v=5-1yXo5zp1I

Produced by the Connecticut Women's Hall of Fame, this six-minute video explores the life and work of Barbara McClintock.

NA, Genetics, and Evolution Documentary
on the Living Science of Evolution

http:///www.youtube.com/watch?v=zSOOcJ_5sVM

Watch this two-hour documentary on DNA, genetics, and evolution.

BIBLIOGRAPHY

"About Pay Equity & Discrimination." Institute for Women's Policy Research. http://www.iwpr.org/initiatives/pay-equity-and-discrimination.

"American Women in World War II." History.com. http://www.history.com/topics/world-war-ii/american-women-in-world-war-ii.

"The Barbara McClintock Papers." US National Library of Medicine at National Institutes of Health. https://profiles.nlm.nih.gov/ps/retrieve/Narrative/LL/p-nid/45.

Barbara McClintock, Pioneer of Modern Genetics. Video recording. Pleasantville, NY: Sunburst Communications, Inc., 1990.

"Barbara McClintock: Statement of Achievements." Statement for the National Academy of Sciences, 1967.

Del Giudice, Marguerite. "Why It's Crucial to Get More Women Into Science." *National Geographic.* http://news.nationalgeographic.com/news/2014/11/141107-gender-studies-women-scientific-research-feminist.

Email from Dr. Maxine Singer to Edith Hope Fine, Mar. 16, 1997.

Fedoroff, Nina. "Marcus Rhoades and Transposition." *Genetics Society of America.* Nov 1, 1998. Vol 150, No 3. http://www.genetics.org/content/150/3/957.

Fine, Edith Hope. *Barbara McClintock: Nobel Prize Geneticist*. San Diego: eFrog Press, 2012.

Gabriel, Mordecai L., and Seymour Fogel. *Great Experiments in Biology*. Englewood Cliffs, NJ: Prentice-Hall, 1955.

"Gregor Mendel: The Father of Modern Genetics." National Institutes of Health Office of History. https://history.nih.gov/exhibits/nirenberg/HS1_mendel.htm.

Hall, J., M. Lee, B. Newman, J. Morrow, L. Anderson, B. Huey, and M. King. "Linkage of Early-Onset Familial Breast Cancer to Chromosome 17q21." *Science*. 1990.

Kass, Lee B. "Records and Recollections: A New Look at Barbara McClintock, Nobel Prize–Winning Geneticist." *Genetics*. Aug 1, 2003. Vol 164, No 4. http://www.genetics.org/content/164/4/1251.full.

Keller, Evelyn Fox. *A Feeling for the Organism: The Life and Work of Barbara McClintock*. New York: Henry Holt, 1983.

Keller, Evelyn Fox. Private interview with Marcus Rhoades, May 16, 1980.

"Kimber Genetics Award." National Academy of Sciences. http://www.nasonline.org/programs/awards/kimber-genetics-award.html.

McClintock, Barbara. "The Significance of Responses of the Genome to Challenge." Lecture given Dec 8, 1983. NobelPrize.org. http://www.nobelprize.org/nobel_prizes/medicine/laureates/1983/mcclintock-lecture.html.

"National Medal of Science." National Science Foundation. http://www.nsf.gov/od/nms/medal.jsp.

"Nebraska Agriculture." Nebraska Department of Agriculture. http://www.nda.nebraska.gov/publications/ne_ag_facts_ brochure.pdf.

"The Nobel Prize in Physiology or Medicine 1958." NobelPrize. org. https://www.nobelprize.org/nobel_prizes/medicine/ laureates/1958.

"120 Years of American Education: A Statistical Portrait." National Center for Education Statistics. http://nces.ed.gov/ pubs93/93442.pdf.

"Program for Andrew D. White Professors-at-Large." Cornell University. http://adwhiteprofessors.cornell.edu.

"Publications of Barbara McClintock." U.S. National Library of Medicine at National Institutes of Health. https://profiles.nlm. nih.gov/ps/access/LLBBHG.pdf.

Ravindran, Sandeep. "Barbara McClintock and the Discovery of Jumping Genes." *Proceedings of the National Academy of Sciences of the United States of America*. Vol 109, No 50. http://www.pnas.org/content/109/50/20198.full.

Rhoades, Marcus. "Barbara McClintock: Statement of Achievement, 1969." Cold Spring Harbor Laboratory Archives.

Segelken, Roger. "Obituary: Barbara McClintock." *Cornell Chronicle*. Sept 10, 1992.

"The Thomas Hunt Morgan Medal." Genetics Society of America. http://www.genetics-gsa.org/awards/thomashuntaward.shtml.

Transcript of Barbara McClintock's Cold Spring Harbor Laboratory press conference, given on Oct 10, 1983.

INDEX

Page numbers in **boldface** are illustrations. Entries in **boldface** are glossary terms.

ABOUT THE AUTHOR

Cathleen Small is an author and editor who has written nearly two dozen nonfiction books for students on topics in the history, literature, science, and technology fields. She has a particular interest in genetics and all things chromosome because her family consists of herself and three chromosomally unique individuals—terms such as "trisomy," "microdeletion," and "chromosomal anomaly" are part of her daily life. When she's not hanging out with her chromosomally diverse husband and sons, she's reading, writing, or traveling.